# TORVER:
## The Story of a Lakeland Community

# TORVER
## The Story
### of a
## Lakeland Community

## John Dawson

## Phillimore

1985


Published by
PHILLIMORE & CO. LTD.
Shopwyke Hall, Chichester, Sussex


© John Dawson, 1985


ISBN 0 85033 567 1

Printed and bound in Great Britain by
THE CAMELOT PRESS LTD.
Southampton, England

*To Arthur*

# Contents

## List of Plates
### (between pages 20 and 21)

1. Anthony Inman cutting nettles with a ley
2. Torver vale from the road to Rosley Thorns
3. The old walled road from Crook to Low Park
4. The road to Scar Head
5. The road to Tranearth and the High Common, showing a ruined hoghouse
6. Looking back to Torver from Eddy Scale quarry
7. The great hole, Bannishead quarry
8. Torver beck, the falls above the mill
9. Torver beck, above the old quarries
10. Torver beck with Dow Crags in the background
11. Beckstones farm with Dow Crags in the background
12. Moving sheep and lambs at Park Ground
13. Park Ground
14. Torver Mill
15. The pool below the mill
16. The yard at Hazel Hall
17. General view of Souterstead
18. Torver from the Whins
19. Looking to the Low Common from the Whins
20. The kirk and the school
21. View from the church towards Emlin Hall
22. The churchyard
23. Looking south-east towards Coniston Water from Cove Bridge
24. Looking north up Coniston Water
25. Garth Nook from the Whins
26. The old wood-working manufactory at Sunny Bank
27. Claude Cann working at Broughton Moor quarry in the 1920s

# Preface and Acknowledgements

The origin of this book is to be found in the walks that Arthur James and I used to take around the parish at the time when the children in our respective families were still too small for hikes over the high fells. In the course of these walks we came upon so many mysterious trackways, apparently leading to no identifiable destination, and the ruins of so many old buildings in the woods and fields, that we decided to give point to our walks by mapping the tracks and measuring the ruins. This fieldwork took us several years of weekend walks in all weathers and gave us a thorough knowledge of the topography of the parish, but not a lot besides. We had become fascinated by the numerous remains we had discovered, and wished we could get to know the people who had built them or lived in them. This wish proved exceedingly difficult to gratify because, apart from the Rev. T. E. Ellwood's two slim volumes written a century or so ago, nothing had ever been written systematically about Torver. If we wanted to find out who these people were, we should have to do some research ourselves.

At this point a sabbatical term at Durham University enabled me to spend some time on research, and I returned home with a file of miscellaneous information to add to our field notes. The two files matched in all sorts of ways. I began to get really involved with Torver, and felt that I was at any rate on nodding terms with some of those Wilsons and Whinfields who had lived here so long ago. Encouraged by Dr. W. Rollinson of Liverpool University Extra-Mural Department, I began to put my material together, did a lot more work in local libraries, and soon discovered that there would be enough to make a book. Torver has been grievously neglected by writers in the past, so I felt I should take the trouble to fill this particular gap. Here, then, is the first full-length book about this Lakeland community, characteristic of others in the area by the stubborn quirkiness of its inhabitants, and the way in which they have created the landscape that in our own day so many millions of people have come to love.

Two people to whom a special word of thanks is due for their contributions are Asadour Guzelian, who took the photographs, and David Macaulay-Allcock, who did the drawings. Their work not only makes the book more attractive to look at, but also conveys a better impression of Torver today than my words could ever do. Finally, my thanks to all those Torver residents who have talked to me over the years, and given me the opportunity to look at documents or buildings not normally open to public scrutiny.

I would also like to thank the following individuals and organisations whose sponsorship made the publication of this book possible: Mr. and Mrs. P. Appleyard, Mrs. I. Barbour, Mr. and Mrs. K. Barrow, Mr. and Mrs. J. M. Bibby, The Burlington

Slate Company, Mr. A. C. Cann, Coniston Co-operative Society, Mr. and Mrs. E. Dickinson, Mr. P. Dickinson, Mr. J. N. Dixon, Messrs. J. F. and E. Hadwin, Mr. J. E. Hellen, Mr. G. Kendal, K Shoes of Kendal, Brig. R. Lewthwaite, Mr. R. Litton, Mr. T. P. Naylor, Mr. and Mrs. R. Prickett, The Provincial Insurance Company, The Rawdon-Smith Trust, Rev. and Mrs. M. Ridyard, Mr. and Mrs. B. Thompson, Whitbread's Brewery, the late Mrs. E. M. Young and Mr. R. A. Young.

The substance of chapter one and part of chapter 14 on slate quarrying have previously been published in *Country Life*, to whom grateful thanks are due.

## Chapter One

# *Torver in its Setting*

The parish of Torver is situated on the west side of Coniston Water. Its lake frontage differs from that of both Blawith to the south and Coniston to the north in being generally steep and wooded, accessible only to the determined pedestrian. The path connecting the pleasant meadows of Water Park in Coniston with the tree-lined shore between Oxenhouse and Brown How is narrow and rocky. One or two barely decipherable tracks run through the woods to the bracken-covered pathless undulations of the Back Common. In the hollows are several shallow tarns; at Long Moss, the largest of them, are the remains of a dam which was once used to regulate the flow of water down Moor Gill to the iron bloomery at its foot. Kelly Hall tarn, on the far side of the common from the lake, is used as a private water supply. There is not, then, a great deal to reward the ordinary walker who forsakes the regular path along the shore.

The other commons continue right to the summit of Walna Scar, south of Old Man. The Low Common begins immediately beyond Torver beck below the farm known as Beckstones, separated by no more than the width of one field from the Back Common, and fills the whole southern portion of the parish as far as the line of settlements – Hazel Hall and Rose Hill – which look down to the Broughton road. This is a desolate area today except for the environs of Torver tarn in its eastern corner. A few trees are struggling to establish themselves hereabouts, carefully fenced to protect them from the omnivorous sheep. The sheep are the principal inhabitants of these commons, responsible for maintaining the land in the state of bleak desolation to which the axes of the woodcutters first reduced it as they fuelled the fires of the bloomery hearths. These sheep are remarkably hardy and athletic creatures. They can be seen pottering about whatever the season, however bitter the weather. In times of famine, late spring in particular, they will come down to the village gardens. At times like this, no wall or fence can keep them out. If it is impossible to scramble underneath or through, they will go over the top. The irregularities of the old stone walls give them plenty of footholds; indeed, they may often be seen in winter time standing on the tops of the walls that are supposed to restrain them, nibbling the bits of vegetation growing there.

The High Common, paradoxically, is less bleak than the Low Common, perhaps because it has been bare of trees for a much longer time, and the brown moorland grasses have covered all the land. This is a wonderful place for the walker, who can turn aside to explore the steep little ravines which the mountain becks have carved into the rock, or go beyond the moor to attain the ridges of Walna Scar or Brown Pike by a final steep scramble. The views from these heights are tremendous, because they are at the edge of the Lake District. In one direction, therefore, are the mountains, in

1

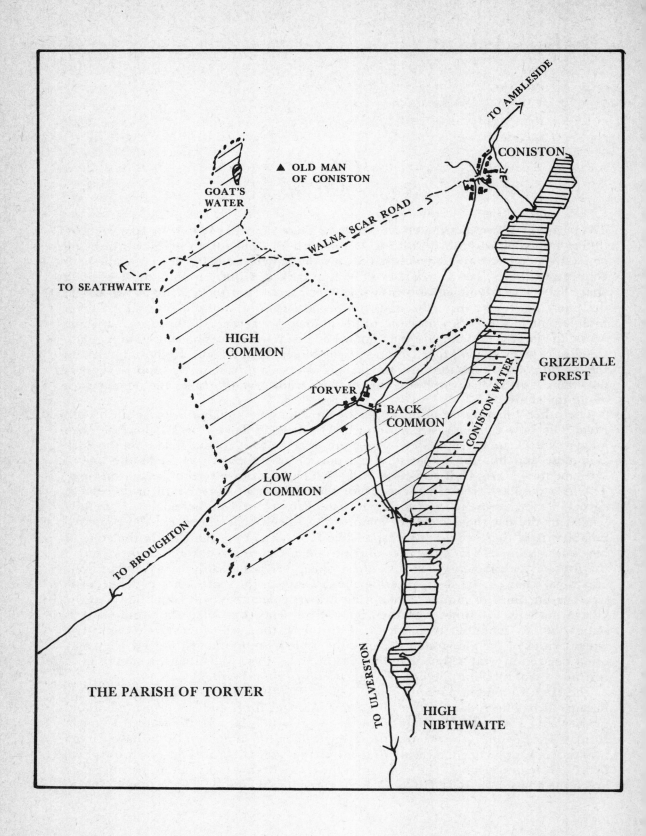

GOAT'S
WATER

▲ OLD MAN
OF CONISTON

TO AMBLESIDE

CONISTON

WALNA SCAR ROAD

TO SEATHWAITE

HIGH
COMMON

TORVER

BACK
COMMON

GRIZEDALE
FOREST

CONISTON WATER

LOW
COMMON

TO BROUGHTON

TO ULVERSTON

HIGH
NIBTHWAITE

THE PARISH OF TORVER

the other, the coastal plains and the Furness peninsula. The presence of the sea adds a further interest to the southern and western outlook even if the day is not clear enough for the Isle of Man to be visible.

The settlement of Torver is situated in the basin of the shallow valley sheltered by the three commons, and created by Torver beck turning aside from the bulk of the Back Common to flow south until it finds a way into the lake round the flank of this obstacle. The impression which the place has made upon visitors has been remarkably varied. G. A. Cooke, who compiled a *Topographical and Statistical description of the County of Lancaster* in the second decade of the 19th century, perfectly illustrates the 'romantick' over-reaction which dated from the 18th-century discovery of the lakes. To him the fells are 'a range of rugged rocks, in a dark semicircle, enclosed by the Conistone fells and the rocks of Tower [*sic*], huge, black and stupendous; while the unexplored mountains of Cove, Rydal Head and others without a name, overtop the whole.'

William Green in his *Tourist's New Guide* of 1819 was anxious to get on to Coniston.

At Oxen Houses the road leaves the Lake, after which for a considerable distance, it is only seen in retrospect ... On the top of the hill [ie. at Emlin Hall], the traveller will find that he has considerably neared the heights of Coniston, which continue in view till he joins at Torver the public road from Broughton to Ambleside; at Torver there is a chapel, and, for refreshment, a decent public house. From Torver to Coniston the mountains are occasionally shut out by intervening pastures and meadow grounds, on which are fantastically situated pretty farmhouses and cottages, beautifully embosomed amongst their native ashes, oaks and sycamores.

The *Complete Descriptive Guide to the Lakes*, published in 1847, was frankly dismissive.

The ancient village, or rather the dispersed assemblage of little farmhouses, called Torver, contains little to interest, except its primitive, un-modernized appearance, which accords pretty fully with the manners and customs of its inhabitants ... Torver Church ... has nothing in architecture to recommend it to notice.

A. C. Gibson in his *Ramblings and Ravings round Coniston* (1849) was more properly appreciative.

There are few places now in England where old-fashioned and unsophisticated manners prevail more decidedly than in Torver ... After noticing the many old , but comfortable and substantial dwellings with which the remarkably verdant fields of Torver – which flow with milk and honey – are bedropt, you must take the road which the guidepost tells you leads to Ulverston: if you can't read, ask at the blacksmith's shop ... and you reach the eminence on which stands the old farmhouse called Hem or Hen Hall.

Gibson has expressed the minority, or connoisseur's view, for travellers in the Lake District have been consistent in ignoring the broad valley through which they passed whenever they rode or drove from Coniston village to the countryside at the southern end of the lake. Let us therefore turn aside, and trace our way, on foot, from the highest point of the parish right down to the shore of Coniston Water. Paradoxically, the remotest and wildest part of the valley is often the busiest, as groups of walkers or climbers make their way to or from the summit of Coniston Old Man or the rocky faces of Dow Crags. The tarn set between these mountains is Goat's Water, and here are the headwaters of the beck. This is no place for the casual stroller, particularly in winter, when fierce winds sweep down from the snow-covered slopes. The rock hereabouts is very dark, almost black, and it is strewn haphazardly about the shore so that even to walk alongside the water is something of a scramble. Looking across to the almost vertical crags, the onlooker will, as likely as not, see and hear the climbers matching their skills against the buttresses and gullies. A melancholy reminder of the stakes involved is the large box immediately below the rock face, at the top of the desolate screes which run down to the water, where the Mountain Rescue team keeps its emergency equipment.

Goat's Water is seldom benign in its aspect and so contrasts the more with the stream which runs out of it, or rather, percolates through the rocks. There is no outlet in the conventional sense, and Torver beck emerges some distance below, where the moor begins. Here we are approaching an area where there has been human activity for thousands of years. Only the hardiest of the old quarrymen going up to Goldscope, farmers gathering sheep or enthusiastic foxhunters had ever left traces of their presence on those terrible slopes at the head of the valley. But on the High Common are many reminders of the old way of life.

The beck, cold and clear, rushes below Cove Bridge, a beautiful stone arch above the roaring waters. This bridge carries the old road over Walna Scar between Coniston and the Duddon valley, marked on 18th-century maps in bold print, and very important to the industrial traffic of the time. For the 20th-century walker there are few more exhilarating ways than this road, from which a panorama unfolds, first over Coniston Water and the rich farmland of the Crake valley, then over more and more miles of wooded fell to a distant glimpse of flat-topped Ingleborough, and the sunlight sparkling over Morecambe Bay. This moor through which the stream passes is now a lonely place, but it was not always so. Small stone circles and numbers of burial cairns remind us of the earliest settlers. The oldest identifiable homestead is on a bluff above the beck. It consists of a low outer rampart and an inner circular wall, presumably the outline of the house itself. This is probably an Iron Age enclosure, for it matches others excavated in South Lakeland.

More mysterious, and possibly dating from the same period, is a long linear earthwork towards the southern end of the moor, marching roughly east-west round the breast of Bleaberry Haws, turning south in a right angle at its western end. Its purpose cannot have been defensive, its line makes no sense as a boundary, so we are left with the suggestion that it may have been an aid to the medieval cowboy rounding up his stock. Certainly, the lowland farmers came to the moor for many purposes. Old, barely perceptible tracks fade into the remains of peat mosses; in living memory the farmers not only had, but used, a peat house adjacent to their yard. Others led to the places on the narrow belt of Coniston limestone where the stone was excavated, and then burnt in kilns which can still be seen. Others again go to the small quarries such as Ash Gill.

The moor indeed is of no less interest to the geologist than to the antiquarian or the naturalist, for there is a great variety of rock formations. The best known of these is the Ash Gill series of fossiliferous Calymene shales, part of the Coniston Limestone series which succeeds the Borrowdale Volcanics.

Having crossed the moor, Torver beck drops steeply into the lower part of the valley through the remains of old coppice woodland, mainly hazel. Until 40 or 50 years ago, these woodlands were systematically managed by their owners to yield a useful crop every 14 years or so. Numbers of pitsteads may easily be identified. These are the circular platforms on which the charcoal burners constructed their fires. The explorer seeking them will be rewarded in season by the primroses and wood sorrel, wood anemones and bluebells; he may well startle a jay or a woodcock, and overhead a buzzard may be mewing. But the woods are steep, rocky and pathless. It is wiser to return to the former packhorse road, and survey the valley as we emerge by one of the farms into open land.

Torver was originally a scattered settlement of Scandinavian farmers, and so has none of the characteristics of the traditional nucleated village. The old farms form a ring round the circumference of the valley, on the slightly higher, better-drained ground. Their fields, separated by stone walls, slope towards the beck, where the church, the smithy, and later, the railway station, were built. The stone walls deserve a study to themselves. The oldest are made from 'cobbles': undressed stones which may well have been gathered from the land which the walls were first built to enclose. Stiles, consisting of three or four flat stones protruding in echelon from each side of the wall, are always sited in conjunction with a hoghole through the wall, for the convenience of the hoggs. This word strictly refers to yearling sheep not yet shorn, but is also used loosely to describe sheep generally. These underpasses are just large enough to enable the sheep to go through one at a time from field to field. A large flagstone is kept at hand for blocking the way when it is desired to confine the stock to a particular pasture. Occasionally a stile consists of a gap in the wall, with two flat pieces of stone inserted so that there is just room for one human foot to pass at the base; at thigh height the stones curve away to the ends of the wall, enabling the rest of the human body to follow the foot, but allowing no passage to a sheep. Here and there are still smaller passageways through the walls, at ground level. These are known as 'smoots'. Their purpose is to help drainage, and also to allow small creatures to pass: very convenient for them, as well as for the man who may have placed a snare to enmesh the journeying hare or rabbit.

For centuries, this was a largely self-sufficient community, sharing belatedly in the prosperity which came to the English countryside during the 17th century. The great rebuilding took place here in the 18th century, and most of the farms now consist of an 18th-century farmhouse, with the older dwelling occupied across the yard by stock, or used for storage. Several such buildings are of the longhouse pattern, with humans at one end, animals at the other, and hay stored on the floor above. In the details of their construction, these often ruinous places display many unusual features of interest to the antiquarian, such as the hooded hearth and fire window. There are no buildings of great architectural distinction, however, and no manor house; but the overall impression is unified, and still not much different from the time when everyone had his patch of arable where he grew the oats to make into haverbread, and everyone kept a few cattle, some sheep, and usually a hive of bees.

Today's traveller will miss the real flavour of the place if he simply takes the insensitive road through the centre of this historic landscape. Only on foot can he continue to follow the stream as it falls away again from the open valley to the later stages of its journey. He will take one of the farm tracks across the fields, beneath ancient hedges of ash, hazel and bird-cherry. If the month is May, the shout of the cuckoo will mingle with the crying of lambs; in winter, snow reveals the tracks of fox or hare.

Soon the traveller is above the mill, beside the falls. These falls pitch the stream headlong 50 feet or more into a gloomy ravine where rowan and birch cling precariously to tiny pockets of soil. The leat used to conduct water from a point above the falls to the mill wheel. Its line can be traced, although the mill, now converted into a house, contains none of the old machinery. This is a very retired spot, and magically beautiful. The stream curves round the building, then below the old stone bridge levels out into the mill dub, an alder-fringed pool where otters could be seen until the mink ousted them, and where in summer local boys will be fishing or bathing.

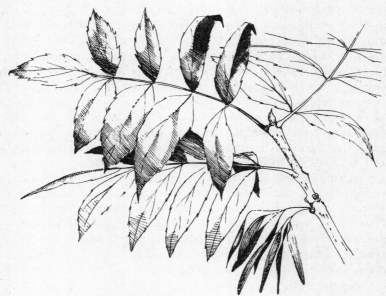

The final stretch of the river is wildly rocky again. On either side, the walls of the valley rise steeply to the lower commons, from which the majestic mountain line of Walna Scar, Old Man and Wetherlam draws the eye and commands the scene. Yet there is matter of interest closer at hand, too. These commons were not always covered with bracken and heather. Until relatively recent times they were wooded, sheltering the Bronze Age people who built their burial cairns there, and later, the iron smelters. Mounds of bloomery slag may still be seen both by the lake shore and on the higher ground. One sited at Gipsy Hollin, evokes by its name the smelters and the vanished trees. The older editions of Ordnance Survey maps mark 'Roman Bloomery', but this is to give the sites an antiquity which almost certainly they do not deserve. Only after the dissolution of the monasteries in the 16th century did the eager industrialists of the day seek to make their fortunes by exploiting the woodlands. The heaps of slag most probably date from this period – those on the remoter parts of the common are very likely to have been the most recently in use.

The iron workers have long ago faded into history, though industrial activity at Sunny Bank, below which Torver beck enters Coniston Water, continued into recent times. The traveller leaning on the parapet of the bridge on a spring morning sees the daffodils strewn across all the gardens and embankments. A dipper hurtling downstream, however, may distract his eye and lead it to the spillway above the water wheel, still housed in the premises which were an important woodworking 'manufactory'. For many years this was the property of Messrs. Richard Charnley & Sons, Pick- and Hammer-shaft makers, and Bobbin manufacturers. Their products included ships' fenders, the market for which was not far away in days when shipping came up to Greenodd and filled the canal basin at Ulverston. In this area also, there used to be a pillbox factory. It must have been a very modest establishment, almost a domestic industry.

The beck has cut its way down through the rock past the mill and Sunny Bank from the wider agricultural part of the valley. Here, where it enters the lake, there is a tiny delta plain, farmed from Oxen House. This is a quite different world from the Wagnerian grandeur of Goat's Water and the far mountain vistas. Snow seldom lies, the early primrose shines from the river bank, the yellow flag and the purple loosestrife follow in their season. The traveller on the bridge will idly watch the red or white sails of little yachts moving along the lake, and speculate what luck the char[1] fishermen in rowing boats may be enjoying. Meanwhile his comrade who chose the higher way may well be battling into the wind, anorak zipped to the chin. That is one of the glories of the Lake District, which the few miles of this little valley illustrate to perfection. Within so short a distance there is such an astonishing variety of scene, and such a remarkable sense of the way in which the heritage of the past is still all around us.

*Chapter Two*

# Prehistoric Times

To walk by one of the vestigial trackways on to the bare and windswept High Common is the only way to see the numerous remains from prehistoric times, which are scattered abundantly on the higher ground above the limits of more recent cultivation. But this is also to gain a false impression of the reality of those days. Five thousand years ago, when the earliest settlers arrived in High Furness, the land was tree-covered almost to the summits of the mountains and the valley bottoms were swampy. With the limited range of tools at their disposal, the only possible place for them to live was on the flatter, more open ground of the Low and High Commons, at, or somewhat below, the 1,000 foot contour. The forest was not so dense at this level, and the narrow belt of Coniston limestone helped by providing a small area of good grazing land. Small parties of nomadic hunters must have passed through at still earlier times, but about 3,000 B.C. woodland clearance began in the fell country on a significant scale. Pollen analysis has shown a sharp decline in elm, oak and pine pollen at that time, as if people were cutting elm branches as fodder for their stock, and clearing trees to create open pastures. Some of the mysterious and apparently quite inconsequential groups of cairns may date from this period, although, if they do represent land clearance, there are now no discernible boundary walls near any of them.

It was not until about 3,500 years ago that the scale of clearance became larger, the first cereal crops were grown, and stone circles constructed, such as the Sunbrick circle on Birkrigg Common near Ulverston. The Torver circles are like most of the Torver cairns, neither immediately spectacular nor obviously datable to a particular period. Two circles are situated on Bleaberry Haws, one outside the angle of the so-called deer dyke, the other within its line. The outside one is more like a ring mound and has a diameter of 53 feet. The inner one is smaller, and not in fact circular. The seven stones have a north-south diameter of 17 feet, and an east-west diameter of 13 feet. H. Swainson Cowper[1] found a rough paving of cobble stones at a depth of two to three feet, resting on the natural rock. The stones, which have an average height above ground of about one foot six inches, are easily found. There is no sign of a ditch round them, and if there ever was a mound in the centre, Swainson Cowper's workmen disposed of it. Probably no mound ever existed. It is difficult to read any religious significance into this little circle, which could well be all that remains of some quite mundane structure, such as a rat-proof storehouse.

Undoubtedly there was increasing activity on the High Common in Bronze Age times. Pollen from Blind Tarn, in the little cwm below the summit of Brown Pike, indicates a significant reduction in the forest cover about 1,000 B.C., but by no means a complete clearance. The land would not have the open aspect that it presents today. The groups of cairns, burial or other, would be situated in open glades or by relatively small areas of cleared ground. Some of the cairns were definitely more than just heaps of stones piled up so as to be out of the way. Swainson Cowper excavated ('ransacked' was the word used by Rev. T. E. Ellwood who was present) the most significant, and largest, set inside the Bleaberry Haws dyke above Bull Haw Moss beck at 790 feet above sea level. This cairn, 36 feet in diameter, had already been rifled before 1887. A quantity of scattered burnt bones suggested cremations, and in a hole of one foot three inches diameter and one foot two inches depth within the circumference of the cairn, and 12 feet east-south-east of its centre, was a considerable deposit of burnt bones, accompanied by the remains of an earthenware vessel, very much decayed and very fragmentary. A. Burl[2] refers to apparently similar holes filled with burnt deposits in the Lake District. Although it was not possible to determine the original purpose of the vessel, it had been ornamented with circular impressions placed in perpendicular rows. Also within the circumference of the cairn, this time eight feet south-west of the centre, Swainson Cowper found a cist[3] of four flat stones set on edge, covered with a large flagstone which measured three feet nine inches at its greatest length and two feet nine inches at its widest point. Inside the cist was a very decayed deposit of burnt bones unaccompanied by any other objects. The only other cairn to have incorporated a cist appears to have been the one near the angle of the dyke. The remaining cairns scattered over the common are no more than heaps of stones, with no sign of cist, surrounding ditch or stone retaining circle.

The most attractively situated group of cairns is the one south-east of Throng Moss on the Low Common. Here the ground rises gently to the north-west. Below, to the south-east, is a swampy depression through which Mere beck flows. The cairns lie in a wide arc looking towards a large glacial boulder on the north side of the beck, marked on the 1845 six inch O.S. map as 'Grey Stone'. The place feels as if it had been inhabited at some time. The big stone is a focal point; near it, the stream has been artificially channelled, for no obvious reason. The size of the nine cairns varies from 10 feet to over twice this diameter. They are such jumbled heaps that it is impossible to come to satisfactory conclusions about them, but the largest are big enough to have been dwellings, and the smaller, storehouses. Sheltered by the surrounding woods and the low ridge behind, with a convenient water supply, and having easy access to Coniston Water for wildfowling and fishing, this ought to have been a very desirable site. But, maddeningly, the stones tell us nothing definite.

The same thought applies to the earth circle which crowns Hare Crag. This is a ring mound approximately 100 feet in diameter. The encircling rampart which is six feet wide has shallow depressions on both its inner and outer sides, each with an average width of 18 inches. The Rev. R. D. Ellwood, fossicking round here, found what he called traces of an ancient burial. Today there is a suspicion of an artificial mound within the circle, raising the summit of the hill (820 feet) by another foot. On the south-east of the perimeter is a gap which may have formed an entrance. It is magnificently situated, with an outlook over Torver valley and the lake, and, in the opposite direction, across the uplands to the wild summits of Dow Crag and Old Man. Nettles grow nearby, suggesting a former human association. The place name itself may be derived from the Old Norse 'horgr', a heap of stones or an altar. A native resident told in 1972 how her grandmother had always regarded it with a certain awe as a holy place, and that she herself had been brought up to believe that it had anciently been a place of worship. But again, maybe it was no more than a palisaded look out to which a few cattle could be driven in an emergency.

Be this as it may, we can be sure that people lived among the fells during the Bronze Age period, clearing the oak forest to provide grazing for their stock. This clearance for stock raising, which prevented regeneration of the woodland, opened up the landscape considerably, and altered the vegetation pattern of the uplands for generations. Since the climate was warmer and drier than it is today, they were able to grow cereal crops in small fields. Between *c.* 800 and 500 B.C., however, the climate deteriorated, allowing the formation of peat on the upland, and the pastoral land use of the deforested areas hastened the impoverishment of the soil. The trend to the present acid and infertile conditions began with those ancient people's sheep and cattle.

At about this time, *c.* 500 B.C., the iron-using Celtic people arrived. Both on Bannishead Moor, just across Torver beck, and on the Hawk, above Broughton Mills, are the remains of their homesteads, stone-walled circular huts within a palisaded enclosure set on a stone-built perimeter dyke. The lack of clear evidence makes it very difficult to distinguish Bronze from Iron Age remains. More important than such labels is that there was continuity of settlement, its extent determined by the successive amelioration or deterioration of the climate.

The Romans called the people who lived here *Brigantes*, and did not bother them much. This was too poor and remote a place to warrant any attention from the usually hard-pressed defenders of the Solway shore. A largely Celtic population, then, lived on throughout the Roman occupation of Britain, sharing its relative peace and prosperity, and enjoying the climatic amelioration which took place from the third to the fifth centuries A.D. There is no record of any battle, or of any Christian missionary in the area. Pollen analysis indicates that there was renewed clearance of the upland oak woods, some of which had regenerated during the previous centuries, and some cereal cultivation. The stimulus for this would have come from the needs of the Roman garrisons and the inhabitants of the civil settlements adjoining the numerous forts in what is now Cumbria. The decline and collapse of Roman rule was a gradual process, and the inhabitants of Torver would scarcely be likely to have noticed the precise moment at which they first owed allegiance to the British kingdom of Rheged.

The arrival of Anglian settlers in Furness during the second half of the seventh century, however, was a portent for the future. The Anglians have not left any clear remains in High Furness, but a few Torver place names have Old English elements in them – the farm known as Souter*stead* for example, and High Stile is situated on the ridge ('stele') overlooking Torver vale from the east. The great movement of peoples throughout Europe continued with the migrations which brought Scandinavians to Furness in the ninth century. The number of place names ending in '-ergh', a hill pasture, such as Torver itself ('Thorvergh' in the Assize Rolls of 1246), suggests that they came from the Hebrides, driven thence by the arrival of fresh waves of their compatriots. Place names containing '-ergh' are not found in Ireland, the other possible jumping-off point for these settlers, to whom the valleys running from the Duddon and Crake estuaries would be a home from home. The established Celtic and English inhabitants were unobtrusively submerged, leaving scarcely a place name behind. In the 10th and 11th centuries woodland clearance for pasture continued, and the farms along the edge of the low-lying ground in the valley bottom were consolidated and sometimes re-named, Scar Head, Crook and Hoathwaite, for example. On the higher ground the settlers marked out and maintained their summer grazing allotments, Bannishead and Eddy Scale.

Prehistory went on for a long time in Torver, but after the Norman conquest the area was at last brought into the orbit of centralised rule, and allocated as the holding of a particular, named person. The earliest extant document, which marks the division between history and prehistory, dates from the 12th century. In 1163 an agreement between William I de Lancaster and the Abbot of Furness partitioned the mountain district of High Furness. William took the western part, which included Torver, and the Abbot the eastern part, beyond Coniston Water. William retained venison and hawks in the whole area, and in return paid the Abbot a yearly service of 20 shillings. At last, real people are materialising from the misty half-light of conjecture. History has begun.

*Chapter Three*

# Medieval People

The historian of everyday places, whose inhabitants have never found fame in national annals, is fortunate if he can find more than the baldest references to specific persons, and then it is usually in legal documents which are apt to show only the more disagreeable aspects of our ancestors. Nevertheless, even a few scanty remains can sometimes light up a situation, rather as scattered sunbeams illuminate the Lakeland landscape on a cloudy day.

Thus, Torver first comes into sight, rather obliquely, in the agreement between the Abbot of Furness and William Fitzgilbert of 1163, confirmed in 1196 before King Richard I's justices at Westminster. The abbot and the baron marked out their respective spheres of influence in the Furness fells, and Torver was part of the baron's share. The boundary ran 'along Yedalbeke to Connyngeston, and so to Thurstaneswatter, and thence by the shore of that lake to the Crayke ...' Hunting and hawking in the area were William's principal concerns, and we may be certain that from time to time the great ones, with their retinues, would cross what we now call Torver common in pursuit of the hart or the wild boar. The scene would be less colourful than those depicted in late medieval Books of Hours, but no less exhilarating in its progress or sordid in its brutal conclusion. The folk who actually lived in the valley no doubt found discreet ways of supplementing their own diet with the fruit of the chase.

For there were people established in Torver at the end of the 12th century. One was Roger de Hedon of Brackenbarrow. He was the son of Augustine, to whom William de Lancaster II had granted lands in Torver earlier in the century. In 1202 Roger was tenant of half a caracute[1] of land, with appurtenances, in 'Thorwerghe'. An assize of mort d'ancestor[2] had been summoned between him and William, son of Waldof, from Ulverston. The outcome was that William quit-claimed, or, as we should say, renounced, his right in the land to Roger and his heirs in perpetuity. In recognition of this quit-claim, Roger gave him 10 marks of silver. This was a fair sum of money. Clearly, Roger was not a toothless peasant huddling in a thatched turf hut. When Gilbert Fitzreinfred came a-hunting, he was not riding through a landscape inhabited only by an occasional swineherd straight out of *Ivanhoe*. Although direct evidence is hard to come by, there must already have been a number of farmsteads in the Torver valley, those on the slightly higher ground forming a ring just above the swampy area where in recent geological times there was a lake.

In the mid-13th century there were certainly enough people for Roger II de Hedon (Heaton) to feel it was worth his while to build a corn mill by the beck, a short distance below the great falls. A mill was not only a good investment, by reason of the tolls which the owner was entitled to levy; it was also a genuine convenience for the

the people who lived nearby. They grew their own 'corn', oats more often than wheat, on which they depended for their daily bread. Unfortunately, Roger's superior lord, William de Lancaster III, already had a mill in Ulverston. His interest was that as many persons as possible should bring their corn here for grinding, even though the journey was long and arduous. So in 1241 (Assize Rolls, 30/31 Henry III) he sent one of his men, Ellis by name, to Torver, with instructions to throw down the mill. No doubt William's lordly authority was a sufficient protection, saving Ellis from the ducking in Torver beck which everyone must have felt he deserved. But Roger did not allow the matter to rest, and in 1246 we find him as plaintiff in a suit against William for having taken forcible possession of a certain water corn-mill in 'Thorfergh', respecting which he claimed that William 'threw down the said mill to the injury of his free tenants in that vill'. It is pleasing to record that Roger won his case. He gave William two marks of silver, and in return received liberty to 'erect and maintain the said mill without gainsay of William and his heirs'. William also quit-claimed Roger and his heirs all right of exacting from them or their men in Torver any suit of (ie. obligation to use) his mill at Ulverston. This was a notable victory, but there must have been a good deal of anxiety over it all, not to say journeys to Lancaster to the Assizes. Perhaps it was the thought of all this that determined Roger to grant the mill to the monks of Conishead Priory not long afterwards.[3] But the wheels went on grinding into the 20th century as the men of Torver made their way along one or other of the numerous trackways which converge on the mill like the threads leading to the centre of a spider's web.

It would be a mistake to think of these farmers as a set of horny-handed but peaceable toilers. They were the fiercely independent descendants of the Scandinavians who had established themselves in this valley, and given most of the farms and natural features their names. From time to time a hand was raised in anger and not all off-comers were protected as Ellis had been by the authority of his own lord. In 1245 William, son of Waldef del Greines, 'killed Henry de Horegrave in Thorvergh fields, and fled'. 'Greines' could just conceivably be the farmstead which later came to be known as 'Grene-rigg'. 'Horegrave' is one of the places in Plain Furness, near to Lindal, where iron ore was already being extracted. The accused, whose chattels were valued at six shillings, was outlawed. Fortunately, most disputes ended less violently, maybe because they concerned land or buildings. At a slightly later date, for example, William de Furness was having troubles with his Torver properties. We find him at odds with the Prior of Conishead in 1252, when there was a writ of Novel Disseisin[4] respecting an unspecified tenement in 'Torwag'; and in 1260 he was claiming 11 acres and a messuage in the village against William de Gresdale. The Stable Harvey people also kept getting themselves into lawsuits over land. In 1314 it was alleged that Henry, who lived there, and his wife Matilda, had taken forcible possession of quite extensive properties in Ulverston. In the end the plaintiff, Richard son of John de Hodeleston, gave them a 'soar'[5] sparrow hawk in return for their acknowledgement of his rights. Then again, Richard, son of Adam de 'Stabilhervy', was involved in 1337 with Richard de Swinbeir, who was claiming land in Torver against him.

All of this suggests that the land must have been good enough to be worth quarrelling over, and indeed some of the landowners must have been fairly substantial men, known at least throughout Furness; Adam himself qualified for the list of those to be included in the Exchequer Lay Subsidy for 1332.[6] Earlier, in 1315/16, there had been an enquiry as to whether it would be to the king's prejudice to allow certain lands in 'Thorvergh' to be given to Conishead Priory. This inquest took place in Ulverston, and the three persons, who between them were giving 60 acres of meadow and wood, were Adam de Clayfe, William of the same, and Thomas son of Gilbert – an interesting comment on the personal links and the comings and goings that there were over the fell trackways in those days. Clayfe, or Claife, is on the high ground overlooking the western shore of Windermere at its northern end, the best part of 10 miles from Torver. The members of the inquest found that:

> it would not be to the prejudice or injury of the King or of others, if the King should grant power to Adam to give 14 acres land, 4a. meadow and 2a. wood; William, 12 acres land, 6a. meadow and 2a. wood; and Thomas, 12 acres land, 8a. meadow and 2 a. wood, to the prior and convent of Conyngesheved and their successors in perpetuity: the premises are held of the prior by fealty [the vassal's oath of fidelity to his feudal lord] and 12 pence yearly to be paid for all services, and worth yearly in all issues 30s. Adam, William and Thomas hold the premises of the prior, and the prior of Sir John de Làncastre, and the latter of the King, in chief: ... one Roger de Heton formerly lord of the said town of Torvergh ... gave the premises to the said prior and convent ...

This is a marvellous example of the feudal chain of land-holding.

In the 1340s we find references to John de Torver. He seems to have had a similar position to that of Roger a century earlier – 'lord of the said town of Torver'. John's affairs give a tiny glimpse of his actual stock and activities. He complained, unsuccessfully, in 1341, that the Abbot of Furness had unlawfully taken six oxen and four cows. Six oxen made up a plough team, and were far beyond the resources of the typical farmer of that time. In 1346 he was one of the jury which testified to the estate of the de Coucys, whose nearest property to Torver was 'certain tenements in Blawith [the adjoining parish] worth yearly 10s. 9d., the pannage of pigs [the right to pasture swine in the woods] worth yearly 3s., profit from the sale of wood yearly 6s.'. These farmers knew as much of their neighbours and kept just as accurate a watch over their activities as do their successors. Part of Torver at this time was included in the estate of John de Haveryngton of Aldingham, a settlement between Bardsea and Rampside on the east coast of the Furness peninsula. When he died in 1347 his properties comprised, *inter alia*, 'a close called Torvergh worth yearly 6s. 8d.; pleas and perquisites of the court there, worth yearly 20s.'. John de Torvergh would have been a member of the court leet jury which made these valuations, but no records of its early deliberations have been preserved.

Yet with an effort of the imagination we may see what it was like in the first half of the 14th century. Let us begin a tour of the parish at Stable Harvey, home of that Adam listed in the Exchequer Lay Subsidy of 1332. This is still one of the principal farms in the area, the old farmhouse and buildings situated above a delightful little secret valley set apart from the main present-day lines of communication. Leading us down the steep wooded slope and across the flatter land by the tiny beck where he grew his oats, Adam would bring us down again to Oxenhouse by the side of Thurston Water. Not indeed to the same farm building that we can see today, but to a dwelling on the site, small we might consider, primitive even, but recognisably the ancestor of the present farm, and no less matched with the landscape: stone, turf and thatch, peat stack and bracken store, byre and barn, and little stone-walled enclosures, punctuated by stiles and hogholes.

A trackway leads us from Oxenhouse by Beckstones to the mill. There is no bungalow half way up the hill, and if we wish to digress on to the common, we shall have to use the stepping stones to cross the swiftly flowing river above its confluence with Mere beck, from which the ghost of a path winds below the oak and holly trees which dominate the woodland. The whole area is much less bare than we see it today, and by the beck are wild daffodils. But we go on past Beckstones along the cartway leading through the ford to the mill. In Adam's time the mill was a tiny route centre, with tracks leading away up the hill to Em How, to the main part of the village along the contour of the hillside west of the beck, and out on to the low common where the gipsies camped. Continuing by the second of these roads, above the river, towards the village, we should find a settlement in almost every place where there is a farm now, reached by little pathways which still largely follow the lines they must have taken then.

We could go first to the south-west corner of the valley, and see how the lambing was going at Souterstead, and then make our way north through the fields immediately below the rocky overhanging hillside, last buttress of the Old Man, squeezing through, or clambering over the stiles by Undercrag to Torver Park. A multitude of lanes spreads out from here across the flat, low-lying land stretching across the valley as far as Hollace. We would very likely have wet feet by now, and we certainly would have by the time we had retraced our steps along Car Lane and then Sattery Lane to the vicinity of the mill. Each of these place names evokes, correctly, the idea of a wet and swampy place. Alternatively, Adam might have taken us on towards Scarhead, where the packhorse way led up to the high common and Walna Scar, and then by Crook to recross the river at Brig House. There would be a farmhouse at Crook, from which we could look towards Coniston over the Little Arrow lands. Once across the river we should be able to visit numbers of Adam's farming friends. At every place where there is now a farm or a ruin of one, there was a dwelling in 1332 – Hoathwaite, Brackenbarrow, Grassguards, High Stile. The basic shape of Torver has not altered over these last six or seven hundred years, and if Adam could come to visit us, he would be able to find his way about with ease. He would use the same roadways between the same settlements. Only the railway terrace and the council houses nearby would be unexpected.

If we look more closely, however, life must surely have been very different. In a sense it was, in that there were few of the gadgets and contrivances which make our life so comparatively comfortable. In a deeper sense, the difference is more apparent than real. Adam de Stabilhervy lived, as does the modern farmer, in accord with the slow rhythm of the seasons. He had to be more self-sufficient, but each is equally bound to the pattern of the farming year.

No buildings have survived from the 14th century, but the oldest existing steadings, including ruinous ones, can give us some idea of the ancient way of life. The scale of buildings was small, because holdings were small and there were no large quantities of anything to be stored. Houses were small too, because they were difficult to build and to heat. Basically, they were places in which to shelter and to sleep, because the routine work involved in mere survival occupied almost all of people's time. The barns were the largest of the buildings, as may be seen, for example, in the ruins of Grassguards. Almost certainly, the usual pattern of the Middle Ages was that still to be seen in the oldest farms, with the barn immediately alongside the dwelling, making a longhouse. There were little stone-walled enclosures round the farm, forming paddocks, and small separate buildings for the varied stock of a self-supporting household: peat house, brackenstore, calf-house, pigsty. Some of these outbuildings would be at a distance from the farm – the hen-house, whose occupants would be very free range, and the hoghouse out in the fields somewhere for sheltering sheep. Once he got used to the absence of labour saving machinery, the present day farmer would find no problems in getting along with Adam de Stabilhervy. He might even find Adam more knowledgeable than himself on a wider range of farm topics, and handier at dealing with whatever situation might arise, because the 20th-century farmer in Torver is not habitually an arable farmer, for instance. He does not normally keep pigs. He does not have to do his own baking, brewing and farm maintenance, as Adam did with the exception of blacksmithing. He does not have to cut and fetch his own fuel. He does not have to spend his time hunting animals and fish, legally or otherwise, in order to supplement his diet.

In the Middle Ages the community as a whole was more self-sufficient than it is today. With travel as difficult as it must have been over rough, usually wet tracks, the establishment of the mill must have been a great boon. At regular intervals the Manor Court met, with the lord's steward presiding. This was the time when many local problems were resolved, on the spot. Sometimes there were disputes over boundaries, or complaints about the miller's conduct. Sometimes a farmer would be given notice that he must put part of his property into better repair, or clear a blockage in a watercourse. The court had the right to levy fines in order to enforce its decisions. There would seldom be any reason or incentive to travel far from home. Neither would there be time, because all the work had to be done by muscle power at walking pace. It would be easy to glamorise all this, and draw highly moral contrasts with our own artificial, mechanical environment, and no doubt there were delightful days, when the sun was shining and the larks were singing above the high common, or the char biting nicely and no-one about to notice the presence of the fisherman. But in general, the toil must have been unremitting, and the work backbreaking, with the climate hostile and the rewards scanty. Adam de Stabilhervy and his contemporaries were still living the same kind of life as their Scandinavian or Celtic ancestors, who had established independent settlements for themselves in the primeval wilderness beyond the bounds of the older lowland and coastal villages.

*Chapter Four*

# Mainly Woodlands

Its woodlands have been for many centuries one of the glories of High Furness, as well as a source of pleasure and profit. As early as the middle of the 12th century, when William de Lancaster made his agreement with the Abbot of Furness partitioning the mountain district of High Furness, he reserved for himself venison and hawks in the whole area in return for a yearly service of 20 shillings. The abbot and monks had second thoughts later, regretting such liberality; when in 1196 Gilbert Fitzreinfred, husband of William's granddaughter, confirmed the agreement, he released to the monks his right of venison and hawks in their part of the fells. As a sweetener, the abbot granted him Ulverston and all its belongings for 10 shillings a year, an interesting comment on comparative values in those days. That the hunting rights were jealously preserved is further illustrated by the terms on which Augustine de Heton held his half carucate of land in Torver in the later part of the 12th century: 'to hold by the service of ¼₈th of a knight's fee[1] for all service, save only to the grantor and his heirs, buck and doe [roe deer], wild boar and sow, wild goat and goshawk ...'

There had to be no impediment to the chase or the free movement of wild beasts, particularly the deer. In the Calendar of Charter Rolls one may note that grants to enclose forest land are sometimes made on condition that a 'deer leap' is incorporated. That to Robert of Abington in 1230, for example, is very specific: 'the enclosure to be done so that beasts of the chase may have free entry and issue'. When John de Hodilliston, lord of Millom in the late 13th century, permitted the Furness monks to enclose pastures at 'Botherhulkil and Lyncove', which lay within his forest in Eskdale, he clearly specified that the enclosure dyke was to be low enough to allow even young deer to leap over it (... *eorum fetus dictas clausturas possint transilire*). Part of this dyke may still be seen, and there may well be a similar structure running across Bleaberry Haws on the moor above Torver.

It could be described as a linear earthwork, the general line of which, running from south-east to north-west, extends from a point on the slope of the hill above Greenrigg, over the summit of the hill (1,000 ft.), down to the swampy valley drained very inadequately by Bullhaw Moss beck, up from this shallow valley on to the top of Bleaberry Haws (*c.* 1070 ft.), finally, to the north-east of the summit, turning at a right angle to the south-west for a final stretch of rather less than 200 yards. The general width of the rampart is about 10 feet, and in places on the north-east side, about two feet high. On the steepest part of the slope from the Moss to Bleaberry Haws a drystone wall, now much scattered, replaces the earthen bank. There is no depression to the north-east of this section, presumably because there was no need to dig down as that was where the earth rampart was built. A curious feature is the

17

presence on the other slope above Bullhaw Moss of a short embankment, making a sort of Y-shape on the south-west side.

This dyke, striding down to the Moss and then marching across the crest of Blaeberry Haws, can be seen from as far away as the lower slopes of Old Man beyond the common. It makes no kind of sense as a defensive line, and has no apparent relationship to the numerous cairns in the vicinity, or to the two small stone circles on Blaeberry Haws. W. G. Collingwood in his *Lake District History* quoted a charter of William I de Lancastre to Roger, son of Orm of Kirkby Ireleth, and dated between 1170 and 1184, which may throw a little light on the structure. The document refers to land between the Licul (Lickle) and the Duden, and:

> from Licul over against the mountain to Deirsgard and from the head of the fence upwards to Calfheud, and thence over the mountain to the head of the valley of Glenscalan to Wranishals [Wrynose], and so by Duden back to the Licul.

Licul, Duden and Wranishals are plain enough on the map; to the walker crossing Broughton Moor from the headwaters of the Lickle, a boundary line to the great dyke, then up to Dow Crag (Calfheud) and on to Wrynose above Seathwaite Tarn valley (Glenscalan), makes satisfactory sense in relation to the land already partitioned between William and the Abbot of Furness to the north and east. All this land was known and used as deer forest and sheep pasture, valued at only four shillings a year, from the early Middle Ages. It would not be so bare and bleak as it is today. The trees would be thinning out on Blaeberry Haws, but there must have been extensive cover for game and scope for pastoral farming. Some of the old place names, Plattocks or Ash Gill, make no sense if the area had been as it is now. The dyke therefore may have been used by those who kept stock on the uplands but, like the one in upper Eskdale, it was not to impede the progress of the chase.

There was plenty of room for everyone then. Stray references in early documents suggest that there were people in these remote parts who by their presence embarrassed the monks – squatters living with their *catalla* (ie. chattels) in the fell country without official approval. Throughout the Middle Ages no-one was likely to come enquiring too closely into everything that was going on. Without doubt the old woodland industries can trace their origins back for more centuries than the existence of documents confirms positively. When records become more abundant, relating to the 16th century, it is clear that the woodlands were still extensive and busy. They played a regular part in the pattern of daily living for the inhabitants, as well as providing an industrial base for the iron smithies.

Some of the regular activities were perfectly lawful. The record of rentals in the Furness Abbey Coucher includes 4d. 'from each tenant in Furness fells who keeps a fire, at Easter, by ancient custom, for greenhew' (ie. cutting the lower branches from the trees). The local pigs were turned loose in the autumn woods just as we see them in some of the illustrations from late medieval Books of Hours. It was a society much more self-sufficient than our own, and with a much more limited range of specialisms. 'Farmers' is not really quite the right word for the people who lived in and around Torver. They were not producing a crop of any kind for the market. Their foremost consideration was the survival of themselves and their families, and so the produce of their land and their beasts was for their own consumption. The only degree of specialisation would derive from a person's particular skill or interest, and here the woodlands played an essential role. A man might obtain a licence from the landlord to cut wood for a variety of purposes, connected with tanning, making ropes or baskets, or such items as 'cartsadles, cartwheles, cardebourdes, cupps or hoopes for cowpers'. This is not to say, of course, that somewhere in Torver there would be a sign over the door of an olde-worlde workshop, 'Joiner and Wheelwright', or 'Swill Basket Maker'. Whoever made these things would do it as a sideline. There was no large market for such products, no means of easily transporting them to where a large market might be supposed to exist. John of the Moor, as it might be, would do his joinery work in the intervals between tending his cattle, sheep and pigs, looking after his land and maintaining his buildings.

However, not everyone's excursions into the woodland were lawful. There was game worth the risk of poaching, and not everyone who wanted to make wooden dishes or baste[2] ropes bothered the abbot for a proper licence. Some people even carried on quite extensive operations. William Sawrey, for example, made a habit of taking 'holyngs, thornes and hasylles' for the 'elyn of asshes'. He certainly wouldn't be able to cut wood and then burn it in a potash pit in some secret little corner. Potash pits are circular in plan, usually of about five feet diameter, and built into the slope of the ground, so that they can be fed from the top side, and ash raked out through a rectangular aperture left in the bottom side. The pit is stone-lined, and curves inwards towards its base, giving a basin shape, as deep as it is wide at the rim. Bracken, rich in potash, or twiggy material, maybe left over after coppicing for charcoal, was burnt in the pit. The resultant ash was raked out and used along with animal fat to make soft soap. This soap was not used for washing the faces of the peasantry, but the cloth they made. There were bigger operations than potash making, notably the activities of the iron industry.

By the 16th century this industry had developed to a degree in which considerable specialisation prevailed. At the time when the Abbot of Furness was taking 4d. from each tenant for greenhew, he was taking £20 from John Sawrey and William Sandes, farmers with three 'smythes' in Furness fells, employed in making iron, for 'licence to get wood and water sufficient to keep up the said smythes'. The enormous bulk of wood needed to produce enough charcoal to operate a furnace ensured that the ore was brought to the woodland for smelting. Thus a tremendous area of coppice woodland was created. This consists mainly of hazel, which is cut down every 15 years or so. The trees grow again from the remaining 'stools', producing another crop of poles ready for the next harvesting. The remaining coppice woods of High Furness are dotted with circular charcoal-burning platforms, 'pitsteads', from which the bags of charcoal would be taken to the rude loading quays for strings of packhorses to carry to the various forges. One such quay may still be seen just above the shore of Coniston Water, not far from Harrison Coppice. To give an idea of the scale of these operations, in 1570 William Fleming of Coniston sold for £280, 2,000 packhorse loads of charcoal to the Governors, Assistants and Comminalty of the Mines Royal.

The forges in which the abbot was interested were at Cunsey (above the western shore of Windermere, just south of the ferry landing), Force Forge (south of Satterthwaite village) and an unnamed place. Sandes and Sawrey were still the lessees at the time of the Dissolution, when, along with a lot of other people, they got a remarkably good bargain. Sandes was to operate the Cunsey forge, Sawrey the one at Force Forge, and the third one they were to take for a year in turn. But two lessees and three forges clearly invites problems, unless the persons concerned work in close harmony. Discord quickly prevailed in High Furness, because in 1549/50 we find Sawrey's widow, Katherine, now married to William Rawlinson, involved in a court case against the heirs of William Sandes, who it was claimed, 'have entered into all three smithies and kept possession thereof'. Maybe the increasing profitability of the iron trade brought out the worst in these people, as they began to see opportunities for becoming rich. Certainly, both families continued to prosper in material terms. A later Sawrey, Miles, was the principal in a group recorded in the *Survey and Valuation of Woodlands* (1610), as holding the largest portion of the Coniston woodlands. There were over 1,000 timber trees, variously valued at 18d. or 2s. each, as well as the same number of short-stubbed and decayed trees (6d. to 8d.), but only 100 saplings.

This looks very like the old story of exploitation, and inadequate replacement of stocks. Indeed, the government of the day had become so alarmed at the denudation of woodlands, caused by the requirements of the iron industry, that a statute of 1564 had placed stringent controls on 'bloomeries'. These were the places at which the iron ore was crudely smelted to produce 'blooms' of low-grade but workable iron. Almost certainly some of the heaps of bloomery slag which may still be seen in what are now apparently the bleakest and most unlikely places, far from any trees, on, say, Torver Low Common, date from these days of reckless boom, and represent the illegal activity of some post-1564 fly-by-night entrepreneur. There is one above Gipsy Hollin, beyond Torver Tarn, and another even farther out, high up the shallow valley of Mere beck. By the end of the 16th century the woodlands had ceased to be part of the basic unchanging background to everyday life, and had become another natural resource to be exploited.

1.   Anthony Inman cutting nettles with a ley. Torver beck is just visible.

2. (*above*) Torver vale from the road to Rosley Thorns. Coniston Old Man dominates the skyline.

3. (*below*) The old walled road from Crook to Low Park.

4. (*above*) The road to Scar Head. Jock Wilson's swill shop was situated under the shadow of the big tree.

5. (*below*) The road to Tranearth and the High Common. Note the ruined hoghouse by the roadside.

6. (*above*) Looking back to Torver from Eddy Scale quarry. Bethecar Moor beyond Coniston Water closes the view.

7. (*below*) The great hole, Bannishead quarry. The field walls beyond mark the Tranearth intakes.

8. Torver beck, the falls above the mill.

9.  Torver beck, above the old quarries. Dow Crags (left) and the Old Man form a majestic skyline.

10. (*above*) Torver beck with Dow Crags in the background.
11. (*below*) Beckstones farm with Dow Crags in the background.

12. Moving sheep and lambs at Park Ground.

13. Park Ground. The small building with the skylight used to be the farmhouse.

14. (*right*) Torver mill.

15. (*below*) The pool below the mill. The characteristic range of farm buildings belongs to the mill.

16. The yard at Hazel Hall.

17. General view of Souterstead, showing how there was often more than one dwelling on a settlement site.

18. Torver from the Whins. Note the walls and hedges of the old field pattern.

19. Looking to the Low Common from the Whins. The line of the old railway is clearly visible.

20. (*above*) Kirk House, the kirk and school—focus of spiritual and social life in Torver for centuries.
21. (*below*) Looking towards Emlin Hall from behind the church.

22.  A corner of the churchyard, shaded by one of the yews.

23. (*left*) Looking south-east towards Coniston Water from Cove Bridge.

24. (*below*) Looking north up Coniston Water from above Sunny Bank.

25. (*right*) Garth Nook from the Whins. A typical ruined farmhouse, although the barn is still in use. Note the fell wall separating the fell from the cultivated land.

26. (*below*) The old wood-working manufactory at Sunny Bank.

27.  Claude Cann working at Broughton Moor quarry in the 1920s. Mr. Cann is riving a piece of slate.

*Chapter Five*

# Tudor Torver

As in the Middle Ages, so in the early 16th century, most of the surviving information about Torver is derived from the records of Furness Abbey. Life in 1523 indeed would have been basically no different from life in 1323 in this high fell country, and the principal worldly interest of the inhabitants still lay in land and its ownership. So, in 1523/4 we find Richard Kerby, on the death of his father, Henry, attempting to establish his title to an unspecified number of acres in the township of 'Torfor' against the Abbot of Furness and others. Richard married Katherine, daughter of John Flemyng, and that the family succeeded in establishing itself securely in the local social hierarchy is proved by the presence in 1585 as a free tenant at the Torver Manor Court of Matthew Kirkbie, 'Gentleman'.

At the dissolution of the monasteries there were numerous cases pending in the Furness Abbey court, and some of them concerned Torver folk. William Ascowe of Marshe Grange was making a claim for money which he had rashly or innocently lent to William Cristoforson of Torver. Edward Dawson of Kyrkeby was claiming 14s. from William Atkinson of Torver for two horses. Dawson was evidently in the right, but had not erred on the low side in his valuation of the horses, since the jury awarded him 10s. The widow of Roger Lancaster and his son Roger were claiming 6s. for malt against Richard Atkinson of Torver. Richard denied the debt, and the jury found in his favour at the court held in Dalton, fining the plaintiffs 2d. for making a false claim. This Richard Atkinson was in 1536 the tenant of Torver mill, for which the annual rent was then 23s. 4d. In those days the miller was involved with the toll payable on malt (moltergrave) as well as dealing with the farmers' corn. The homager or, as we should say, tenant farmer, of 1536 could not adjourn to the Kirkus for a draught bitter or a can of lager, so he did his own brewing as well as his own baking. As late as the 18th century many people kept a supply of malt, as may be seen from the inventories of its early decades: 12 out of 32 record malt in the list of personal effects.

It will be noted that two of these three cases concerned Atkinsons. So also did a transaction of 1572 when John Atkinson, son of Will Atkinson, late of Souterstead, released

> a parcel of ground called Brokylbank Ground [this is now the next farmstead north from Souterstead] of the yearly rent of 18d., and 3d. for an intack,[1] and 2d. for a rent called walk-mill silver, being all 23d. per annum, unto William Fleming Esq. and his heirs.

A walk-mill or fulling mill is involved in the process of making woollen cloth. The woven material is soaked in a soapy solution and pounded with feet or hands before being stretched on tenter hooks in the fields to dry. As a result of doing this, the length of cloth has more 'body' and is less liable to shrink. The field above the mill in the direction of Park Ground is still known as 'Tenterbank'. Torver mill is most unusual in that it combined corn grinding and fulling on the same premises. As late as 1911, when the building was for sale, the agent's particulars refer to 'All that Corn and Fulling Mill'. The fact that there are three storeys suggest that the fulling, which is otherwise undocumented, took place on the topmost floor. However, almost half the population of Torver seems to have consisted of Atkinsons in Elizabethan times. Seven out of 15 homagers at the 1585 court leet, and seven out of 14 in 1591 were named Atkinson. It is really therefore by weight of numbers that they figure largely in the records of misdeeds.

Some of them did not look after their property carefully enough, and the Manor Court tried to chivvy such folk. Thus, in the 1580s, Thomas Atkinson of Souterstead and George (his son, or possibly his brother) were required to 'have the gate [ie. track] through Brakenslacke from Bore and to Lyninge gape unto Arnacrag[2] in such sort as their elders occupied the same', upon pain of any that try to stop them to forfeit 40s., a surprisingly heavy fine. It is not immediately apparent why anyone should have wanted to stop them, unless there had been a surreptitious blocking of a right of way by persons unknown. The fact that the place names are not now identifiable does not make it easier to sort out the rights and wrongs of the situation. Other court entries reinforce the impression of great concern over trackways and watercourses. In this rainy district a blocked drain could cause a piece of good arable or pasture land to be flooded to its lasting detriment. For example, it was ordered that the water 'between Ornall Cragg and Brackenslacke shall be kept in the right course, and all other waters in Torver, under penalty of 3s. 4d.'. It was also ordained that 'no person is to cast in or put into any running waters or wells any dead corpse or carcase of any manner of beast', under penalty of 6s. 8d. We must remember that there were no deep freezes in those days, and a dead beast was perhaps too valuable to waste (braxy mutton); or maybe they were just wanting to keep a carcase to feed to hounds at the proper time.

Then the jury meeting in October 1585 ordered John Atkinson of Torver Park to 'sufficiently repair' a barn of his before Whit-Sunday next, or be subject to a penalty of 6s.8d. This was quite a routine entry, but John Atkinson appears again in circumstances which make it less surprising that he should have allowed his barn to fall into disrepair. He had to cope with a most unruly son, named Myles, who had been burning and breaking down hedges, cutting down neighbours' woods, and killing and hurting their goods and cattle to the extent that the court ordered Elizabeth, his mother, 'not to harbour or lodge him after the feast day of St. Andrew next', unless he was able to put in two sufficient sureties that he would desist from this kind of behaviour. Maybe John had given up his son as a bad job: certainly it was not a case of Atkinsons against the rest, because the three men who had suffered particularly from his activities were John Atkinson (probably of Undercrag, the adjoining farm), James Atkinson and John Ashburner.

This John Atkinson of Undercrag was an even more difficult, not to say spiky and truculent character. Along with his father, Richard, he controlled the mill at this time, and they were neglecting it. The story, as revealed in the court records, might have come straight out of Chaucer. In 1585 the court required them to put into the mill 'an able sworn miller by Christmas day next' and that 'no woman shall keep the said milne, upon pain of 40s.'. The same requirement occurs twice more, with a further caution against boys or under-millers. It looks rather as if the Atkinsons were trying to extract maximum profit from the mill, regardless of maintaining it in good condition. They were instructed to put into order the outwheel of the mill, the ring and the meal ark; they were begged for a third time to instal 'an able sworne miller', and urged not to keep the mill themselves. When in the end they did appoint a miller, he turned out to be a rogue, and the next request was that he should be 'expulsed and excluded from the said mill before the 11th of November next', under penalty of 40s. One can imagine the Atkinsons, father and son, having a coarse laugh together over this. They had no intention of obliging the court, and had probably chosen this man, Barker by name, because of his bad qualities. The court indeed had brought a definite case against him – stealing 'one hoop[3] and a half of skillinge[4] corn from Myles Oxenhouse at the mill'. 'Let him', says the magisterial note, 'be apprehended by the Cunstables and brought before some justice of peace'. It was easy to say this, because the hapless constable was the one who would have to try to translate the wish into fact. The note about the Atkinsons' reaction to the request to replace Barker with a more suitable miller is almost pathetic by contrast: 'we find that they have not put in any sworn milner according to this order.'

Some of the farmers, however, were getting tired of this ineffectual shadow boxing, and it may well not be a coincidence that at this time John Atkinson was involved in an affray with Rowland Atkinson, a more senior member of the tribe, and, on the evidence of Christopher Atkinson and Robert Addyson, fined 3s. 4d. It was not simply that the actual milling arrangements were unsatisfactory. The Atkinsons, as moltergraves, were entitled to levy a toll varying from a quarter of a grain to a hoop, according to the quantity of malt that a customer required, and they did not keep proper measures. In fact, they were becoming steadily more awkward, if not positively bloody-minded. They began to refuse to grind the corn and grains of the homagers, and, disregarding the instructions of no less a person than the steward of the manor of Michelland (Michael's land, or, more usually, Muchland, of which Torver formed a part), 'did wickedly abuse the said tenants of Torver ... by violently taking from them for their malt toll so much of the ground corn as did amount to more by the one half than of right was due to them'. There were ugly scenes at the mill. Anyone who questioned or resisted the imposition risked a beating. Thirteen named farmers, including six Atkinsons, affirmed on oath that they had been abused by father or son.

> Or else at the least they the said Atkinsons did refuse to grind their corn even at all, whereby a great number of the said homigers, being buyers of their corn and very poor people, were inforced either to beg or else to have been famished by the scarcity ... of this last summer.

During that particular summer it was all especially galling; the year had been so unusually dry that Torver was one of the few mills in Lancashire with enough water to keep its wheels turning.

John Atkinson was more unhelpful than ever when he was advised by some of his kinsfolk and friends to 'use himself more orderly'. He merely answered saying, 'I care not for the Steward nor Jury, who he then wished had kissed his briches.'[5] In fact he seems to have gone out of his way to be as difficult as possible. On being presented before the court for 'felling and spoiling Her Majesty's woods most wilfully', and being advised to forbear to do so, 'he said and sware that he would fell and take at his pleasure, in despite of who sayed nay'. Then he erected a house on the queen's pasture, and had to be told that it must be removed before the next court, under penalty of 6s. 8d. But neither fines nor requests seem to have had the least effect, and the last extant entry in the court records (1591) is almost the same, word for word, as the first entry in 1585: 'that Richard and John Atkinson shall put and bring one able milner into the milne ...'

Fortunately, most people had a proper respect for the manor court. For example, when it was noticed that a fine house in the holding of Richard Park was fallen into decay, he was required to 'make the same tenantable before the feast of St. Michell next'. A note is appended that the house was 'duly repaired and new builded'. And even if some people did go out of their way to upset the harmony and well-being of the community, there was a more cheerful side, even to being one of the court jurymen, because it was the custom that 'the bailiff of Torver shall make a court dinner at every Court in Torver to the steward, clerk and jury'.

*Chapter Six*

# Local Responsibilities

A considerable effort of imagination is required to appreciate the extent to which the old pre-industrial society regulated its affairs on a very local basis through the unpaid performance of a host of minor public offices by most of the inhabitants of a parish.

The activities of the manor court provide one long-standing illustration of this point. The court is a very ancient institution, with responsibilities relating to the proper observance of the customs of the manor, especially as they concern the transfer of property, and the resolution of petty disputes and annoyances. Documentary evidence is distressingly scarce, but for a short period of the late 16th century, Mr. E. Walker copied extracts from the records.[1] (v. Transactions, Cumberland and Westmorland A. & A. Society, vol. LVII N.S.) The lists of jurymen's names survive for the years 1585 and 1591, dividing the jury into seven free tenants and 15 homagers. The most difficult problems that the court had to deal with between these years concerned the mill, but there was a great variety of other matter, bearing on the efficient and peaceable continuance of relationships within the community.

The jurymen recorded their confirmation of the legal inheritance of property – in 1585, that James Oxenhouse is dead, and that his brother John is his proper heir, who shall pay a yearly rent of 4d. An account of the customs of the manor of Muchland,[2] dating from the reign of Elizabeth I, sets down that a tenant, on being admitted to his tenement, pays to the lord of the manor two years' rent, over and above the usual annual rent. In 1588 the jury presented Thomas Peale 'to be next heir unto one half of one messuage called Bankend by surrender made by Rowland Atkinson of the yearly rent of 12d.'. It is interesting to note that this function of the court continued into the 19th century. A copy of the admission of Robert Lindow Carr to certain tenancies in the year 1820 retains in its wording a strong flavour of ancient tradition.

> At this Court [meeting at Torver Church House] it is presented by the homage aforesaid that Robert Carr gentleman, late a copyhold tenant of the said Manor, died seized of [ie. in possession of] three closes or parcels of copyhold land situate near Sunnybank, commonly called or known by the names of the Acres, one dale or moiety of a close called Beckfoot by estimation half an acre near Sunnybank aforesaid, and half an acre of meadow ground or thereabouts in Torver Church Meadow ...

The yearly rent for these scattered pieces of land was 8¼d., and the fine which Robert Carr Jnr. had to pay for admission was 1s. 5½d. The reference to Church Meadow indicates the continuing division of the 'town field', situated by the river immediately below Hollace Bridge, into small sections, separated by 'meer stones'. (cf. Mere beck which flows into Torver beck above Sunny Bank, and has for centuries formed the boundary between the parishes of Torver and Blawith.)

More picturesque than the routine preoccupation with tenancies are the glimpses which Walker's transcriptions give of everyday life in the village. The jury had to see to it that land and property were kept in decent order, and that no-one by careless or anti-social behaviour endangered the security of either. They had a responsibility for maintaining public rights of way, or customary privileges relating to the woodlands and commons. They were involved in personal disputes when these erupted into public affrays. The troubles at the mill during the later 1580s meant that they had plenty to do under this last heading. An unusual illustration of their less contentious role is concerned with the security of farm buildings, at that time often thatched, from fire: 'we ordain that manner of person or persons shall carry without [ie. outside] any house neither day nor night time fire, but such as shall be closely covered in a vessel, within the space of four hundred foot of any house, sub pena 20s.'

A further sample look at the court records for 1662 shows that the preoccupations and problems did not change. John Crowdson the elder had been putting too many sheep on the common. Also they had to order 'that none shall crossdrive the fell with their goods, but every tenant shall drive his goods from his driftway or outrake straight up towards the height of the fell, and not to cross any "anshent heause" upon pain of 6s. 8d. every default.' The incident when the jury presented William and Isabell, children of Myles Wilson, for stopping of James Brocklebank's goods in the highway going to the pasture is a further illustration of the quarrels that would arise so easily when scarce resources had to be husbanded for the benefit of all.

Resort to physical violence continued to be much more common than it is today. The wife of Richard Parke had been throwing stones at the wife of Robert Wilson. Roger Atkinson (the same name as the minister at that time, but not identifiable with certainty as that worthy) was presented for a hubbleshaw[3] upon Myles Wilson. Edward Jackson and Robert Graves were jointly presented for a bloodwick upon each other, against pain of 3s. 4d. This was in accordance with the usual tariff. Amongst regulations relating to Furness dating from the late 16th century, quoted in the *Lonsdale Magazine* for 30 April 1882, is the following, evidently very applicable to Torver: 'Item: that no person within this Lordship make any fray, on pain of 6s. 8d.; nor bloodstroke, on pain of 3s. 4d.; nor shall unlawfully chide, on pain of 1s.; nor make tuxhill or hubbleshowe, on pain of 1s.; nor for break, on pain of 3s. 4d.' Doubtless the circumstance that so many of the villagers were directly involved in some capacity in keeping the peace helped to contain turbulence and disputes within manageable bounds. In 1662, for example, 16 householders held some office in the service of the court, ranging from the two constables to the pairs of pinders, one for fell and one for field.

In addition therefore to his service as a member of the Court Baron jury, the Torver farmer was expected to take his turn of duty as pinder, hedgelooker, constable, surveyor of highways, churchwarden or overseer of the poor. All these were voluntary part-time jobs undertaken on a yearly basis. The pinder was responsible for the village pound where stray animals were kept until claimed. The Torver pound is no longer visible, but it was situated by the roadside beyond the big sweep of the road at Hollace, above the town field. The hedgelooker's duty was to check that boundary hedges were being kept in good condition, properly layed and clean-bottomed. Hedges still belong specifically to one or other of a pair of neighbours, and if a hedge is your responsibility, you must keep it stock-proof. When the stock in question consists mainly of rough fell sheep, this duty is not light. These two offices, pinder and hedgelooker, have left no records, because no cash had to be accounted for at the end of the year. Some records, however, survive from the constables' accounts (for 1759-1815), and from the surveyors' (for 1768-1853). Most of the farmers took their turn in carrying out these duties, which fell into a pretty regular and predictable pattern.

Although the constable is in no way comparable to the traditional village 'bobby', either in the scope of his authority or the range of his duties, his accounts are always headed by warrants, which involved sums ranging from £1 3s. 5d. to 2s. 9½d. There is nearly always an item, 'Poor Passengers', at about two shillings. In 1768, for example, 'To two companies of poor passengers – 2s. 4d.'. Often money was paid out for ravens (4d.), or foxes (2s. 6d. in 1765, and 3s. 4d. in 1784 for a fox cub). These entries are not so numerous as to suggest that either ravens or foxes were a serious pest, and seem to indicate further that organized systematic foxhunting as it is known in the second half of the 20th century was not then carried on. The likely pattern would be that the farmers gathered each with his own dogs on an agreed date at times when foxes were making themselves too obtrusive. John Peel is credited with the idea of keeping a pack of hounds together permanently, around the turn of the 18th century. The 'poor passengers' are also intriguing. The entry for 1798 says bluntly, 'vagrants', but one would love to know who these people were and where they were going. Then there are miscellaneous entries which refer to the constable's day-to-day concerns. 'I can't hand over swills in that condition', or 'When are you going to get the pinfold gate put right? Those sheep got out of it again last night', or 'Hammer, where can that hammer be? I know there's supposed to be a hammer, but I can't find one ...' To wit,

| | |
|---|---|
| 1761 | To repairing swills 4d. |
| 1763 | To pinfold gate 12s. 1d. |
| 1763 | To hammer 3s. 8d. |

Regrettably these accounts become briefer and more formal in the 19th century, until they disappear in the Victorian rationalisation of local government. The surveyor had more to do than the constable in most years, before he too was incorporated in a County Council department. He 'disbusted' (splendid and regular Torver variant of, presumably, 'disbursed') monies for a variety of purposes:

| | |
|---|---|
| 1769 | Getting conduit stones, and leading[4] 16s. 6d. |
| 1770 | Stone hammer, mending 1s. 6d. |
| 1803 | A guide post 19s. |

These were the days when road repairs usually consisted of breaking stones from small handy roadside quarries into a suitable size for filling the potholes. The accounts show us the going rates for various kinds of work – in 1787, nine pence for a man for half a day, and 9s. 6d. to Martin Dixon for five days' work and 'leading samel'. Samel is the phonetic spelling of the word still used locally for the clayey soil that used to be put over pitsteads, and was used also for binding the road metal.

Rates for the more specialist aspects of roadmaking were agreed beforehand with the contractor concerned. For example:

| | |
|---|---|
| 1770 | To John Tennant and partner for 135½ rood of road @ 1s. 2d. per rood £7 17s. 7½d. |
| 1777 | To Thos. Wilson for 55 rood fence £2 15s. |
| 1778 | To John Bainbridge for gravelling 4½ rood of road at Hummers 6s. 9d. |
| 1823 | To George Fleming for re-walling 226 yards of wall £2 7s. 6d. |

Hummers, high above the village on the way to Broughton Moor and Broughton Mills, crops up with unexpected frequency (in 1772 they had had to spend £6 1s. on repairs to Hummer Bridge), so this road must have had relatively a far greater importance than it has today.

The surveyor raised the money for his expenses by a precept on all householders: 59 of them, for example, in 1774, with their contributions ranging from £1 7s. 6d. paid by John Birkett to 2s. each from Esther Roach and Alex Muligin. This is the first of several appearances that Alex makes in various parish documents. He must have been an immigrant odd-job man who had been around for a long time, and who was too useful or too good-natured to be got rid of, even though he could be a bit of a nuisance. In 1783 the surveyor paid £4 11s. 9d. in cash to Alexander Milligin for making 100 rood in the new Walney Scar road.[5] But clearly he was not regularly employed in honest work. A document of 1784, signed by Edward Parke, churchwarden, and J. Fearon, overseer, records, 'for avoiding further trouble and expense', that Alexander Milligin belongs to the parish of Torver. Ten years later he was still there, in and out of work, receiving 1s. in the overseer's disbursements.

The overseer and the churchwarden were the two most important of the old-time voluntary public officers, at any rate until the spate of modernising legislation that began in the 1830s. From that time on, administration became more centralised and more precisely linked with an all-embracing structure of local government, so that the overseer for Torver was no longer a Torver man taking his turn at the job, and the churchwarden became purely a church officer, whose duties even in this more limited sphere were much less colourful. By 1905 he was concerned not at all with either bell-ringing or dog-whipping, but had to be paying bills for coal and lamp oil, and settling accounts with the organ blower.

# Specimen of Constable's Accounts

1784 Then did William Stilling being Constable for Mr. Nelson's Estate at Grovesground give up his accounts to the Assessors as followeth:

|  |  | £ | s. | d. |
|---|---|---|---|---|
| 1 | Warrant | 3 | 6 | 7 |
| 2 | Do. | 2 | 17 | 1 |
| 3 | Do. | 1 | 8 | 1½ |
| 4 | Do. |  | 17 | 10 |
| 5 | Do. |  | 1 | 0 |
| 6 | Do. | 1 | 10 | 5 |
| 7 | Do. | 1 | 8 | 0 |
| 8 | Do. |  | 12 | 10½ |
| Ten journeys | |  | 10 | 6 |
| Assessors journeys | |  | 5 | 0 |
| (Illegible) windows | |  | 1 | 0 |
| Spent at Sessing[6] | |  | 1 | 0 |
| taking accompts | |  | 1 | 6 |
| a Sess Bill | |  |  | 6 |
| 4 Ravens | |  | 1 | 4 |
| a Fox cub | |  | 3 | 4 |
| Spent at Sessing Con (?) | |  | 1 | 0 |
| To poor passengers | |  | 2 | 6 |
| | | 12 | 19 | 7 |
| | Sess Bill |  | 1 | 0¾ |
| | | 13 | 0 | 7¾ |

# Specimen of Constable's Accounts

1764 Thos. Brocklebank being Constable in the year 1764 gave up his accompts to the assessors as followeth:

|  |  | £ | s. | d. |
|---|---|---|---|---|
| Militia Recept | |  | 1 | 0 |
| 1 | Warrant |  | 12 | 1 |
| 2 | Warrants |  | 6 | 6½ |
| 3d | Do. | 1 | 6 | 7 |
| 4th | Do. |  | 2 | 8¾ |
| 9 Journeys | |  | 9 | 0 |
| Surveyor | |  | 4 | 0 |
| his journeys | |  | 4 | 0 |
| Keeping accompts | |  | 1 | 6 |
| A sess Bill | |  |  | 6 |
| 20 poor passengers | |  | 3 | 6 |
| School lock mending | |  | 1 | 8 |
| a pair tongs ⎫ | |  |  |  |
| Highway hammers ⎬ | |  | 1 | 0 |
| laying ⎭ | |  |  |  |
| spent | |  | 1 | 0 |
| | | 3 | 15 | 1¼ |
| | |  | 4 | 6½ |
| | | 3 | 19 | 7¾ |
| Thos. Brocklebank | |  |  |  |
| Collected | | 3 | 16 | 4 |
| Disbusted | | 3 | 15 | 1¼ |
| Rests | |  | 1 | 2¾ |
| also powder ½lb. | |  |  | 7½ |
| | |  |  | 7¼ |

## Specimen of Highways Accounts

1770 Then did John Brocklebank of Moor being surveyor of highways give up his accounts of his Disbustments for the last year as followeth:

|  | £ | s. | d. |
|---|---|---|---|
| Paid to John Birkett left in arrear | 2 | 12 | 1¾ |
| To John Tenant and Partner for 135½ Rood of Road @ 1s. 2d. per Rood[7] | 7 | 17 | 7½ |
| To Anthony Smith for 14 rood of Road @ 1s. 6d. | 1 | 1 | 0 |
| Spent at setting Road |  | 1 | 6 |
| Spent at making rate |  | 1 | 0 |
| Paid to Mr. Bell for a Rate 6d. and 2d. paid out |  |  | 8 |
| Spent on workmen when I paid them |  | 1 | 0 |
| For dismissing Office |  | 4 | 0 |
| Four journeys to Ulverstone |  | 4 | 6 |
| Stone Hammer mending |  | 1 | 8 |
| To John Fearon, Thos. Wilson, Thos. Atkinson and John Fearon Man, each 2 days work at conduits |  | 7 | 3 |
| 2 days leading coverstone |  | 2 | 0 |
| Disbusted in all | 12 | 14 | 6¼ |
| Received by Bill | 14 | 14 | 5 |
| Remains unpaid | 1 | 19 | 10¾ |

## Specimen of Highways Accounts

1778 Money disbusted by George Ashburner Surveyor of the Highways for the year 1778 viz:

|  | £ | s. | d. |
|---|---|---|---|
| To Thos. Wilson in arrears last year |  | 8 | 5½ |
| Spent at Compounding and 3 Sale Notes |  | 3 | 6 |
| Spent at Setting Road |  | 12 | 4 |
| To William Birrel for 41 Rood ½ Road | 3 | 10 | 5 |
| To   Do.   for gravelling 106 Rood | 5 | 6 | 0 |
| Spent upon workmen at sundry times |  | 3 | 6 |
| ½ day at Hummer lane |  |  | 9 |
| To John Bainbridge for gravelling 4½ Rood of Road at Hummers |  | 6 | 9 |
| To John Rigge for 3 Rood and 6 yards of Stone Fence at 1s. 4d. per Rood |  | 5 | 2 |
| Paid to Mr. Bell for writing[8] |  | 1 | 0 |
| To John Brocklebank for his fence not yet errected | 1 | 6 | 6 |
| To dismissing my office and 1 journey |  | 3 | 6 |
| Total | 12 | 7 | 10½ |
| Due to Geo. Ashburner from new Overseer John Atkinson | 2 | 5 | 3¼ |

*Chapter Seven*

# The Poor Law

The Elizabethan Poor Law was a wonderful example of the old English tradition of placing responsibility for the administration of a system squarely on the shoulders of those who were most closely involved in each locality. In a reasonably stable and simple society this kind of arrangement worked well. It was efficient, because it was in everyone's interest to see that it was so; it was economical, because most of the administration was through unpaid public service.

The Torver overseers' accounts, which have survived from the late 17th century onwards, show the kind of detailed personal concern that was exercised. Many of the items are not specific to particular families, but tell us something about the food or clothing of ordinary people at that time.

| | |
|---|---|
| 1694 | for flesh 3s. |
| | for one peck of bigg [a kind of barley] 1s. 4d. |
| 1698 | one pair clogs 2d. |
| | one winding sheet 2s. 6d |
| | for burying 10d. |
| 1699 | one hoop of potatoes 4d. |
| 1701 | for butter and milk twice 6d. |
| | one day work of peats 8d. |
| | flesh to the poor 2s.3d. |

Sometimes the entries give very personal details.

| | |
|---|---|
| 1699 | to John Dixon for one shirt 1s. 2d. |
| | one hoop of meal to Widow Dixon 3d. |
| | to John and Dinah for cloaths 1s. 6d. |
| | for Thomas Dixon burial 2s. |
| | one coat to Dinah Dixon 2s. 3d. |
| 1701 | Dinah Dixon, for clothing 10s. 3d. |

The Dixons were a family with whom the overseer had considerable and regular dealings, for these are not their only appearances in the records.

Since they were custodians of public money, actually held as cash by themselves, the overseers had to be sure not only that they noted every least transaction, but also that they obtained satisfactory receipts for the monies that they paid out. Two widely spaced fragments illustrate this point clearly – '15th April, 1701: Received of John Atkinson Overseer the sum of five shillings in full of all demands till this time by me'. The signature, in a different hand, is that of Mary Brockbank. Then, from 1804, 'postidge for letters from different places 2s. 11d.'

31

The lengths that successive overseers were prepared to go to ensure that they were seen to be as fair as was humanly possible in the execution of their duties may be gathered from a memorandum inscribed at the foot of the accounts for 1712:

> That Elizabeth Harrison being an old woman past work, therefore the town thought it convenient to let her go about from one house to another according to their rates after the rate of 2d. per day. Now when Providence ordered to remove her out of this world (she at first begun at Milne and left at Brocklebank Ground), they thought it requisite to make this conclusion, that if ever there was another of the same nature they should begin where she left.

A glance at the accounts a century later shows this same concern for detail, and the personal, individual touch. These people had played in the beck together as children, had grown up within the same community, had rejoiced and sorrowed together over many decades. Consider old Edward Atkinson, for example, in 1804, when the overseer paid Thos Wilson 1s. 6d. for repairing Edward's watch, and John Kendal 6s. 'for attending Edward Atkinson, and medson'. For these years in the early 19th century, the accounts list the monies 'disbusted' by the overseers in respect of services rendered :

1814            John Dixon (descendant of John and Dinah?)
                one peck tallos 1s. 4d. (tallows, ie. cheap candles)
                one cart of sods 2s.
                leading 12 carts of peats 6s.
                clogs, cloging 1s.

Since all the payments in relief of poverty had to be made from cash raised locally through the poor rate, the overseers were meticulous to ensure that no situation arose in which they were called upon to pay out money that should really have been found by colleagues in some other parish. Throughout the period of the old Poor Law every 'settlement' was the subject of rigorous scrutiny. In this rather specialised context, a settlement means that a person has established the right to be accepted as a member of a particular community, normally the one into which he/she had been born. A settlement paper of 1724/5 bound the churchwardens and overseers of Cockermouth to take back, if ever he should become chargeable, John Atkinson, weaver and comber of wool, who had removed himself to Torver 'for the advantage of his trade'. In 1730/1 the Torver Court Baron consulted Mr. Gibson, 'an experienced Lawyer', in the following circumstances:

> A person by name Isaac Gillbanck of Broughton, to enlarge his farm, has taken to himself another estate at or under the sum of £9 per annum in Torver. He holds both farms and the rents united together may amount to the sum of £16, or upwards. The said Isaac hath (until three weeks ago at the most) been an inhabitant upon that farm in Broughton but now is removed unto the farm he holds in Torver, and although the man be not yet indigent, yet we the inhabitants of Torver, endeavouring to take all possible care to prevent the said Isaac's inhabiting amongst us without bringing a certificate of whether or no the law will allow him to inhabit in whichever division (Broughton or Torver) he pleases.

One would hope that a person who was able to take on the responsibilities of a second farm was not likely ever to become a pauper, and clearly Mr. Gibson felt that the Torver statesmen were being unduly sensitive. 'As he is of credit to farm £16', he replied, 'he'll scarcely be judged likely to be chargeable so as to be removed at present.'

Nor was Gibson sympathetic to the second inquiry from the Court Baron, which was as follows:

> There was an order enacted by the jury At our Court Baron holden in October last, (which is of the same custom with the tenure of Muchland in Furness) that no person or persons should take to farm a part or parcel of an estate together with a dwelling house under ten pounds per annum, and should ['not' crossed out] be admitted to inhabit there unless the person or persons so farming would procure a certificate of their settlement from such divisions as they belong unto, and we humbly desire to know whether or not the law will permit us to put such an order into force.

The terse reply to this piece of special pleading was: 'I am of the opinion that this order is invalid and not of any avail in law'. There seems to be more than a suspicion that Gillbancks was for some reason *persona non grata* with the natives, who were neglecting no opportunity to make things difficult for him.

Many of the persons that the overseers had to deal with were of course difficult in one way or another. Take Agnes Vicars, for example. In 1759, at the general quarter sessions of the poor at Lancaster, Myles Sandys and James Machell (both justices of the peace from north of the Sands) made a settlement order in respect of Agnes, 'a poor person', out of Hawkshead into Torver. She did not allow the grass to grow under her feet during the ensuing years, and occupied her time to such purpose that in 1769, on 16 December, we find Thomas Park acknowledging from James Bigland, overseer of the poor in Torver, 'the sum of £2 6s. in full for Agnes Vickars and her two bastard children, board, and for performing the midwife's office to the said Agnes'.

There were other difficult ladies, like Ann Whaits (local people still pronounce the surname now spelled Thwaites in the manner of this phonetic spelling). She had been living in Kendal before 1781, but in that year her luck, or the patience of the Kendal overseers, ran out, and a complaint was made to the justices of the peace that:

> Ann Whaits, a woman of ill name and fame, is come to inhabit in the said burgh of Kirkby in Kendal, not having gained a legal settlement there; ... and that the said Ann Whaits is likely to be chargable to the said burgh of Kirkby in Kendal: We the said Justices upon due proof made thereof, as well upon examination of the said Ann Whaits ... do adjudge the same to be true.

And having concluded that her legal settlement was in Torver, the justices required the churchwardens and overseers of Kendal 'to convey the said Ann Whaits from and out of the said burgh of Kendal, to the said township of Torver and to deliver her to the Churchwardens and Overseers of the Poor there', as if, indeed, she were a piece of baggage.

Lest these cases should give the impression that 18th-century Torver was largely inhabited by loose women, it is fair to record how in 1775 James and John Kirkby of Hawkshead were bound as apprentices to John Fearon of Torver, waller. Regrettably, James promptly got a local girl, Agnes Dockray, with child, instead of devoting all his attention to walling, as brother John presumably was doing. Apprentices, girls as well as boys, were another class of person with whom the overseers were habitually involved, although never in large numbers. An early example dates from 1730 when William Wilson, the churchwarden, and James Park, the overseer, placed Agnes Gibson, alias Jackson, 'a poor child of the said parish, apprentice to John Atkinson'.

In return for her promise to serve faithfully and obediently, John pledged himself to teach Agnes 'the art and mystery of huswifry', and to provide her with adequate board and lodging for the term of her apprenticeship, and as a farewell bonus at the end of it all, 'double apparel of all sorts, good and new (that is to say), a good new suit for the Holy-days, and another for the Working-days'.

An apprentices' register covering the years 1806 to 1829 lists only 11 names, of whom one was bound apprentice within the parish, to Moses Harrison the miller in 1809. The destinations of the rest tell us something of the variety of local industries at that time, and the size of the area within which communications made easy contact possible. They were indentured respectively to a waller in Coniston, a dyer in Millom, a tanner in Lowick, a calico weaver in Hawkshead (two), a cotton spinner in Backbarrow, a swiller (ie. maker of swill baskets) in Cartmel, a waller in Cartmel and a bleacher in Ulverston. The 11th is illegible. James Coward's indenture to William Matthews, dated 1818, survives. It is considerably less picturesque than Agnes Gibson's had been, and to that extent speaks eloquently of the change in social climate over a century. The churchwardens and overseers

> do put place and bind James Coward aged fourteen years, who is a poor child of the township of Torver, and whose parents are not able to maintain him, as an apprentice to the said William Matthews, and with him as an apprentice to dwell and serve from the day of the date hereof, until the said James Coward shall come to the age of twenty one years ... And the said William Matthews ... shall and will receive and provide for the said apprentice during his said apprenticeship according to the form of the statutes in such case made ...

Although the earlier document had also been cast purely in the regular form, somehow it gives a more caring impression, and has the stamp of a less hurried age, when people had the time to think of even a poor child of the parish as an individual, who one day would need some decent clothes in which to go out into the world.

After the new Poor Law of 1834 the overseers' accounts became, predictably, more impersonal and less interesting to the historian. The 1851 accounts may serve as a typical example of the newer, more clinical and business-like regime. Payments in relief of poverty to the 'outdoor poor' are listed thus:

| | | |
|---|---|---|
| Joseph Braithwaite | age and infirmity £4 13s. | |
| Hannah Dawson (Coniston) | sickness £4 1s., 2s. 11d. in kind | |
| Agnes Woodend (Hawkshead) | shortsighted £2 14s. | |
| Joseph Wilson | weak mind £3 0s. 9d. | |
| Eleanor Brocklebank (Coniston) | widow with children £1 3s. 6d. | ditto in kind |
| John Danson | want of employment 1s. | |

In addition there was the expense of 4s. 6d. to non-resident paupers, and £9 17s. 2d. to the 'maintenance of lunatics in asylums', a phrase with rather chilling overtones. Possibly there was no less care and attention given to those in need, but the system had become, and has remained, less local in the detailed working of its administration.

### Torver Apprenticeship Indenture

This Indenture made the fourteenth day of May in the third year of the reign of our sovereign lord George the second etc ... Witnesseth that William Wilson Churchwarden of the Township of Torver in the county of Lancaster James Parke Overseer of the poor of the said Township by and with the consent of His Majesty's Justices of the Peace for the said County ... by these presents do put and place Agnes Gibson alias Jackson a poor child of the said parish, apprentice to John Atkinson, with him to dwell and serve from the day of the date of these presents until the said apprentice shall accomplish her full age of twenty one years ... During all which term, the said apprentice her said master faithfully shall serve in all lawful business, according to her power, wit and ability; and honestly, orderly and obediently in all things demean and behave herself towards her said master and all his during the said term. And the said John Atkinson ... doth covenant ... by these presents, That the said John Atkinson the said apprentice in the art and mystery of Huswifry shall teach and instruct, or cause to be taught and instructed: And shall and will, during all the term aforesaid, find, provide and allow unto the said apprentice, meet, competent, and sufficient meat, drink and apparel, lodging, washing and all other things necessary and fit for an apprentice. And also shall and will so provide for the said apprentice, that she be not in any way a charge to the said parish, or parishioners of the same; but of and from all charge shall and will save the parish and parishioners harmless and indemnified during the same term. And at the end of the said term, shall and will make, provide, allow, and deliver unto the said apprentice double apparel of all sorts, good and new, (that is to say) a good new suit for the Holy days, and another for the working days ...

(Abbreviated slightly for ease of reading. Signed, 1730, by the Justices, Messrs. Knipe and Sandys.)

### A Settlement Order, 1781

... Upon the complaint of the churchwardens and overseers of the poor of the burgh of Kirkby in Kendal aforesaid, in the said county of Westmorland, unto us ... that Ann Whaits (a woman of ill name and fame) is come to inhabit in the said burgh of Kirkby in Kendal, not having gained a legal settlement there, nor produced any certificate owning her to be settled elsewhere; and that the said Ann Whaits is likely to be chargable to the said burgh of Kirkby in Kendal: We the said Justices upon due proof made thereof, as well upon the examination of the said Ann Whaits upon oath as otherwise and likewise upon due consideration had of the premises do adjudge the same to be true; and we do likewise adjudge, that the lawful settlement of her, the said Ann Whaits, is in the said township of Torver in the said county of Lancaster. We do therefore require you, the said churchwardens and overseers of the poor of the said burgh of Kirkby in Kendal, or some, or one of you, to convey the said Ann Whaits from and out of the said burgh of Kirkby in Kendal, to the said township of Torver, and her to deliver to the churchwardens and overseers of the poor there ... And we do also hereby require you the said churchwardens and overseers of the poor of the said township of Torver, to receive and provide for her as an inhabitant of your said township.

(Signed by Messrs. Miller and Hadwin, two of His Majesty's Justices of the Peace.)

*Chapter Eight*

# Wills and Inventories

So little light is shed on the everyday lives of our ancestors by formal documents of state, that even the feeble glimmers cast by the few documents which they created themselves is most welcome. A study of 33 inventories and seven wills of folk who lived in Torver in the late 17th and early 18th centuries helps a little in bringing to life that final period before the old ways began to dissolve under the corrosive influence of the industrial revolution.

The slow build-up of prosperity which had begun during the 17th century was being consolidated. Most of the farms in the parish were reconstructed or wholly rebuilt about this time, and life was a little less hard than it had ever been previously in this area. The inventories reveal this prosperity in a number of ways. Four people owned a clock. Robert Fleming's, of Souterstead, was valued at £2 10s., over three times the value of any of the others. John Birkett of Crook had 'an old watch', valued in 1740 at 10s. 6d. Twenty-three persons had brass and pewter to be valued, ranging from £3 10s., that of the successful farmer and businessman, William Fleming of Undercrag, to seven shillings, formerly the chattels of Thomas Atkinson of Greenrigg, whose meagre effects also included '2 pack cloths – 1s. 6d.'. Although the inventory describes him as 'yeoman', Thomas had no farm animals or equipment. He may well have been what we should call a general labourer, or even odd-job man. Everybody had basic domestic equipment and furnishings, even if it was only a bed and table. Poor Mary Atkinson's, of Undercrag, were valued at only 18s. 6d. in total, and it wasn't as if she had only herself to provide for. More often, however, the list goes on from beds and bedstocks to include chests, stools, dressers, cupboards and cushions. The fact that floor coverings are never mentioned suggests that everyone still used dried brackens from the fellside, or rushes. The apprizers of Miles Wilson's estate in 1687 even itemised girdle, brandreth (a stand, usually of wood, for putting a cask on), and frying pan. A chair of his was listed separately; by contrast, a generation later, chairs were not uncommon. James Bigland of that next generation, who died at the mill in 1739, was comparatively well-off. In addition to his bedsteads and bedding, he had a chest of drawers, a table and a chest in the parlour, a chest and a box, a looking-glass and six chairs in the middle room, and two chests and two chairs in the third room. There were also two silver cups and three silver spoons, the disposition of which James carefully specified in his will.

Bigland was unusual in having a 'third' room. The more typical arrangement of the houses is illustrated by the account of Richard Low's possessions, from one of the Stable Harvey cottages. Instead of being itemised separately, his belongings were grouped according to the room in which they were left, thus:

36

Goods in the fire room £1 10s.
Goods in the buttery 5s.
Goods in the chamber 5s.
Goods in the buttery loft £1
Goods in the house loft 10s.

The fire room was on one side of the hall passage as a person went in at the door. The fireplace in this room, against the gable wall, was the heart of the house. Within its great hood mutton would be smoked; people alive in 1980 remembered the flavour with nostalgic relish, knowing they would never be called on to eat it any more, and recalled how huge logs would be fed gradually into the fire by a shove of the boot. The big iron cooking pot would hang over the fire – there was a broken one amid the ruins of Little Undercrag in the 1970s. Then let into the thickness of the wall near the fireplace would be a little cupboard for storing salt and spices. Often an additional little window in the front wall of the house, known as the fire window, gave extra light to the person at work by the fire. The bread cupboard in which the haverbread, made from oats, was stored sometimes formed part of the wall partitioning the fire room from the passage. The oak partitions, still in situ at Park Ground in the late 1970s, although rough, were comfortable-looking. Inside the hall passage were stored all manner of domestic and farm gear, especially the kind that lent itself to being hung against a wall. The smaller chamber on the other side of the passage was either for sleeping, or was, in the tradition maintained in many working class households in Lancashire as late as the 1930s, used only on special occasions, and not normally heated. The buttery was a tiny cool dark space often incorporated below the stairs; the staircase would form a projection from the centre of the back wall of the house. Within this projection it would turn back on itself as it climbed to the sleeping accommodation in the roof space of the house. Where no staircase existed a ladder gave access to the loft, known then as now as the 'cockloft'.

The inventories were 'apprized', or valued, by three or four neighbours, who sometimes signed their names at the foot of the paper. Taking the inventories together with the wills, there are only nine marks, among them, James Bigland's. This seems to indicate that the parson had not striven in vain when the village children came to the church for instruction. Eight of the inventories moreover specify books, none by name except a Bible on a couple of occasions, and never altogether worth more than 10 shillings, except, perhaps, William Fleming's of Undercrag in 1713. His books were listed with a cupboard, and, less explicably, a grindstone, at £1 10s. These statistics at least indicate that Torver was not an ignorant and unlettered community, lacking both the means and the will to learn.

As one would expect, almost everyone was in some way involved in farming, because the community had to be practically self-sufficient for its everyday needs. Only four men, including James Pritt, a weaver of Grassguards, are credited with no agricultural effects whatever. The farming had to be arable as well as pastoral. Bigg, a kind of barley, and oats, hay and straw, are regular entries. Flax must also have been a common crop. Nine of the inventories include references to it in some form; James Bigland, for example, had 'five hanks of linin yarn' in that middle room. Then there were the animals, often a pretty motley collection, no doubt. Anthony Atkinson of Bank End (1743) had 'sheep of all sorts', value £12. Mary Atkinson, a widow from Undercrag, left behind eight sheep valued at £1 12s. The cattle, 'beasts', they were called, then as now, were sometimes grouped as oxen or heifers (whies), but seldom precisely numbered. James Bigland had six, 'old and young', valued at £11, along with 42 sheep, £5 – a scraggier lot than Mary's, one would therefore think. However, this kind of valuation would imply that the bigger farmers, like William Fleming, owned considerable flocks. £22 could mean upwards of 150, in addition to which he had sheep at Turner Hall and Undercrag at Seathwaite in Dunnerdale, both lots valued at a further £10.

The smaller farmers usually kept no more than half a dozen beasts, 'house cows', which would ensure a regular supply of milk for making cheese and butter as well as for drinking. From their sheep they could expect little more than mutton for smoking above the fire, and occasional pocket money from the sale of wool at Kendal market. It was on his way back from selling wool that an 18th-century farmer of Beckstones is supposed to have been inadvertently murdered by neighbours who had intended no more than to knock him senseless so that they could rob him. The echoes of this deed still reverberate, for there are persons who knew nothing of the story, but have heard the startled gallop of a horse in the late evening, when there has been no horse nearby. Most people did own one, or even two, horses, and in the apprizers' entries here we may sometimes catch the inflexion of a voice, the echo of an affectionate relationship. Daniel Fleming, who died at Undercrag in 1731, and whose books included a Bible, had had 'a little mare', and Thomas Walker of Greenrigg (1718) 'an old mare'. There is only one reference to swine, and five to poultry, always with a tiny valuation, such as Miles Wilson's, at one shilling. Bees are more commonly listed, eight times, and were more valuable. Robert Fleming's, at Souterstead, were worth 10s., more than the price of a couple of sheep. Maybe the hens scratched round the barnyards as self-perpetuating flocks which belonged to the household in general rather than any particular person. The bees lived in straw beeskeps that were placed in square recesses built into a suitable wall. These may be seen at several farms, eg. Tranearth, and were still being used for their proper purpose at Beckstones in the 1920s.

The farm equipment was as miscellaneous as the stock. The headings are usually 'horse gear' and 'husbandry gear', with valuations ranging from 1s. 6d. (Rowland Atkinson at Undercrag in 1698) to William Fleming's £1 14s. 4d. for the horse gear and £1 10s. for the husbandry gear. Ploughs are sometimes itemised and twice, wimbles, or wombles. These were instruments turned by a handle, for boring holes in soft ground. In 13 of the yards or barns there were piles of loose wood and boards, and in 17, heaps of sacks and pokes. Two of the farmers must have been actively involved in the woodland industries. Robert Fleming who died at Scarhead in 1729 had a stock of bark worth £1 6s. 8d., and William Fleming, who owned the large flock of sheep, was also into tanning in a big way. He had a stock of leather valued at £64 7s. 6d., and a quantity of horns, hair and bark worth £7 10s.

The most general activity recorded in these inventories apart from farming was spinning and weaving. Fifteen of the 33 folk had stocks of wool, including John Fleming of Church House, the village blacksmith. Of the others, Thomas Atkinson, for example, had two pairs of weights and one wheel; Miles Wilson, wheels and cards; David Fleming, one spinning wheel. Then there were the people whose property included special equipment related to their own trade. Such was Thomas Walker, house carpenter, whose tools, with other iron gear, were deemed worth 6s.

8d., along with board and all other wood, £2. James Bigland bequeathed to his eldest son, another James, various items connected with the mill – mill picks, one stone hammer, and so on.

All these little glimpses add up to quite a complicated picture of economic activity. Maybe Walker, the house carpenter, just did odd jobs for the other Torver folk, but the £64 worth of leather at Undercrag presupposes contact with a much wider market. In fact there must have been much more coming and going than is often appreciated. John Atkinson of Hoathwaite, who died in 1726, was eighth-part-owner of a ship, the *Anna*. The list of debtors and creditors is more wide-ranging than might have been expected. Quite apart from William Fleming, whose business activity must have involved him in dealings with numbers of 'off-comers', or David Fleming, saddletree maker, to whom money was due from persons in Bootle, Hawkshead, Keswick, Ireby, Wigton and Ulverston, Nicholas Browne, husbandman, of Oxenhouse, had £55 9s. owing to him from 15 people, of whom no more than half a dozen can fairly be described as local, in amounts varying from £1 to £13. At a time when the banking system that we take for granted today simply did not exist, people in places like Torver had to make what arrangements they could amongst themselves to accommodate their financial problems.

These inventories, then, reveal a society that was fairly complex, but linked together by common ties of economic self-interest and immemorial custom, with its priorities firmly fixed by the necessity of making a living from the land. It must have been a hard life, but not so hard as to be one long joyless grind, and perhaps it was more attuned to the values of eternity than our own materialistic round:

> In the name of God, Amen. I, Myles Fleming, ... Husbandman, being somewhat infirm in body, but of perfect mind and memory praised be Almighty God for the same ...

## Will of Mary Atkinson 1712/3

In the name of God Amen. I Mary Atkinson of Undercrage in Torver in the parish of Ulverston and county of Lanikester widdow, beinge weekly in boody but perfect in memory praysed be Almighty God for it, doe make this my last will and Testement as followeth: first I comit my soule into the hand of Almighty God hopeinge by the merrits of Jesus Christ my saviour to have free pardon for all my sins, and my bodey to be buried in a Christian manner as my Execitor thinketh fit. And as for my worldly goods such as the Lord hath possed me with, I bestow them thus as followeth.

First I give to Mary Russall my granddaughter the summe of eight pounds. Itam I give to Rodger Atkinson my naturall son one shillinge. Itam I give to James Russall of Backbarow and Agnus his wife either of them one shillinge. Itam I give to Beniamen Atkinson my naturall son one sillinge. Itam I give to Georg Towers of Yudall one shillinge. Itam I give to Agnus Atkinson of Undercrage. one shillinge. Last of all I make Thomas Wilson my son in law my whole Execitor of this my last will and testament, payinge my just debts and legisis and funarell expensis. In wittness hearof I have hearunto set my hand and seall the nineteenth day of March in the year of our Lord God 1712.

Test

John Atkinson Jun.

Edward Jackson

Mary Atkinson
her mark and seall

## Will of Myles Fleming 1731

In the name of God Amen. I Myles Fleming of Scarehead in Torver in the parish of Ulverstone and County Palatine of Lancaster, Husbandman, being somewhat infirm in body, but of perfect mind and memory, praised be Almighty God for the same, yet calling to mind the mortality of my body and knowing that it is appointed for all men once to die, Do make, ordain, constitute and appoint this my last will and testament in manner and form following: that is to say, Principally and first of all I give and humbly recommend my soul into the mercifull hands of Almighty God who gave it, stedfastly hoping through the merits, death and passion of our ever blessed redeemer Jesus Christ, to have full and free pardon and forgiveness for all my sins, and to inherit everlasting life: and my body I commit to the earth from whence it received its originall, to be buried in decent Christian burial at the discretion of my executor hereinafter mentioned, nothing doubting but at the generall resurrection I shall receive the same again by the unlimited power of God: and as touching the disposition of such personal estate as it hath pleased Almighty God to bestow upon me in this world, I give and dispose thereof as followeth: First it is my will and mind that all and every one of my just debts and funerall expences be fully paid and discharged; Item I give unto Thomas Fleming my son two shillings and sixpence in money, all the rest and residue of my goods, chattels, utensills and household stuff of what nature kind or property soever, the same be or found to be appertaining unto me, I do give and bequeath unto my son William Fleming, now of Scarehead in Torver in the parish and county aforesaid, and him only I constitute and appoint full sole and absolute executor of this my last will and testament: he paying all my just debts legacies and funerall expences, and I do hereby utterly and totally disallow revoke and disannul all and every other former wills or testaments by me in any ways before nam'd will'd or bequeathed, ratifying and confirming this and none other to be my last will and testament, hoping all things herein contain'd will be faithfully fullfill'd according to this my will and mind abovementioned and declared. In witness whereof I have hereunto set my hand and seal, this the eighteenth day of May in the fourth year of the reign of our most gracious sovereign lord George the Second, by the grace of God of Great Brittain France and Ireland King, Defender of the Faith &c. and in the year of our Lord God one thousand seven hundred and thirty one.

Signed sealed published and declared by
the said Myles Fleming the testator to                          Myles Fleming
be his last will and testament in the
sight and presence of us whose names are
here subscribed; viz.

Thomas Birkett
William Birkett
John Hall

Whereas in Mary Atkinson's will, written down by a neighbour, Edward Jackson, we can hear the inflexions of a voice through the phrasing and the spelling, in this will of Myles Fleming the curate, John Hall, was trying a shade too hard to make it all sound proper and to render it the more legally watertight by a superabundance of repetition. Yet after all this verbiage, he has said very little, and has even managed to leave a doubt whether the religious phrasing at the beginning is not just a flowery form of words. We may question whether Myles, whose signature is in a very old-fashioned and shaky hand, was overly impressed.

## Inventory re. William Fleming 1713

A True and Perfect Inventory of all the Goods and Chattels, which formerly did belong to William
Fleming of Undercragg in Torver lately deceased as they were prized by us whose Names are hereunder
written this twenty second day of April, Anno Domini 1713

|  | £ | s. | d. |
|---|---|---|---|
| Imprimis/ | | | |
| For Purse and Apparel | 10 | 0 | 0 |
| Item For Bedding and Bedstocks | 2 | 10 | 0 |
| Item for Earthen and Wooden Vessel | | 13 | 4 |
| Item for Brass and Pewter | 3 | 10 | 0 |
| Item for a Clock | | 13 | 0 |
| Item for Iron Gear | 2 | 0 | 0 |
| Item for Chests and Boxes | | 13 | 4 |
| Item for Meal, Malt and Salt | 1 | 10 | 3 |
| Item for Bigg and Oats | 1 | 10 | 0 |
| Item for Sacks and Pokes | | 13 | 4 |
| Item for Wheels, Stools and Chairs | | 3 | 0 |
| Item for Wool | | 7 | 0 |
| Item for Husbandry Gear | 1 | 10 | 0 |
| Item for Gun and Preaper [sic] | | 6 | 8 |
| Item for Bees and Poultry | | 6 | 4 |
| Item for Hay | | 3 | 4 |
| Item for Leather | 64 | 7 | 6 |
| Item for Horns, Hair and Bark | 7 | 10 | 0 |
| Item for Boards, Ladders, loose Wood, Weights and Scales | 7 | 0 | 0 |
| Item for Saddles Ropes and Manure | 1 | 14 | 4 |
| Item for Hemp and Flax | | 8 | 0 |
| Item for Cupboard, Books and Grindstone | 1 | 10 | 0 |
| Item for Seed and Ardor[1] | 1 | 19 | 0 |
| Item for Bease[2] and Horses | 32 | 1 | 8 |
| Item for Sheep | 22 | 0 | 0 |
| Item for Sheep at Turner How in Seathwaite | 10 | 0 | 0 |
| Item for Sheep at Undercragg in Seathwaite | 10 | 0 | 0 |
| Item for Wood | 30 | 0 | 0 |
| | 215 | 0 | 1 |

| | £ | s. | d. |
|---|---|---|---|
| (Individual details omitted of) Money Due to the Deceased | | | |
| upon Mortgage (two persons) | 65 | 0 | 0 |
| upon Bills and Bonds (eight items) | 45 | 11 | 1 |
| Book Debts (forty four persons) | 109 | 1 | 1 |
| Add | 215 | 0 | 1 |
| Totall | 434 | 12 | 3 |
| Funerall Expences & Debts | 46 | 13 | 6½ |
| Clear Goods | 387 | 18 | 8½ |

Prizers
William Whinfield
John Fleming
James Wilson
Edward Parke

## Inventory re. Nicholas Browne 1715

A true and perfect Inventory of all the goods and chattels, quick and dead, of Nicholas Browne late of Oxenhouse in Blawith in the parish of Ulverstone deceased, as they were prized by us whose names are hereunto subscribed, this twenty seventh day of September Anno Domini 1715.

| | £ | s. | d. |
|---|---|---|---|
| Imprimis | | | |
| Purse and apparel | 2 | 10 | 0 |
| Item Horse and furniture[3] | 1 | 1 | 6 |
| Item Brass and pewter | 1 | 0 | 6 |
| Item Iron gear | | 18 | 0 |
| Item Wooden and earthen vessel | | 13 | 4 |
| Item Bedding and bedstocks | 1 | 13 | 4 |
| Item Chests arks and boxes | | 13 | 4 |
| Item Chairs, stools, table & frame | | 10 | 9 |
| Item Cushions and woollen wheel | | 1 | 8 |
| Item Books | | 1 | 3 |
| Item Axes, wimbles and husbandry gear[4] | | 12 | 0 |
| Item Wooll and hemp | 1 | 13 | 4 |
| Item Sheep and bees[5] | 12 | 0 | 0 |
| Item Beasts[6] | 12 | 10 | 6 |
| Item Hay and corn | 5 | 0 | 0 |
| Item Fuel for fire[7] | | 3 | 4 |
| Item Peck & houp[8] with all odd things | | 6 | 8 |
| Totall | 41 | 9 | 6 |

(List of money owing to the deceased omitted.)

Prizers
Wm. Whinfield
Matthew Coward
Test. Jno. Stoup Curate

## Inventory re. Anthony Atkinson 1743

A true and perfect Inventory of all and singular the Goods Chattels and Credits of Anthony Atkinson late of Bank End in Torver in the Parish of Ulverstone and County Palatine of Lancaster Waller, deceased, aprais'd the nineteenth day of March in the year of our Lord one Thousand Seven Hundred and Forty Three by John Atkinson, William Whinfield, Richard Lowther & William Atkinson as followeth:

| | £ | s. | d. |
|---|---|---|---|
| First of all his Horse Purse and Apparel[9] | 10 | 0 | 0 |
| Also his Books | | 5 | 0 |
| Also Bedstocks & Bedding of all Sorts | 1 | 1 | 0 |
| Also Brass, Pewter Wooden Vessel & Earthen Ware | | 15 | 0 |
| Also Sacks Baggs, Wheels Wool & Hemp | | 15 | 0 |
| Also Kitchen Utensils | | 15 | 0 |
| Also Chests, Boxes Tables Chairs Forms & Stools | | 18 | 0 |
| Also Houshold Provision of all Sorts | 1 | 10 | 0 |
| Also Husbandry Gear of all Sorts loose Wood | | 6 | 0 |
| Also Corn & Hay | 1 | 1 | 0 |
| Also Bease[10] | 7 | 10 | 0 |
| Also Bees | | 5 | 0 |
| Also Sheep of all Sorts | 12 | 0 | 0 |
| Also Debts owing to the deceased | 129 | 5 | 0 |
| In all | 167 | 5 | 0 |
| Debts and Funeral Expences | 12 | 0 | 0 |
| Rests | 155 | 6 | 0 |

Apraisors
Wm. Whinfield
John Atkinson
Richard Lowther
Wm. Atkinson

*Chapter Nine*

# A Community Under the Microscope: Torver 1700-1750

Although it is not possible to find out much about everyday activities in Torver during the years when the first two Georges reigned, one can set down a fair amount of information about who lived where and sometimes what public duties each person performed. All the farmsteads, with the possible exception of Tranearth, were in existence, and often each farmstead was a complex of several separate dwellings.

Greaves Ground was the home of the Wilsons, 'Willyam and Elenor', whose initials are carved on the old offertory box in the church. Their son, 'Willyam', was baptised in 1701, followed after a surprisingly long interval by Joseph in 1709, Mary in 1711 and Miles after another long gap in 1718. Willyam the elder figures in 1715 as a member of the Court Baron jury, meeting in the Kirkus; by 1720 the son Willyam was evidently married and still living at home, because in that year 'Elianor', daughter of William and Mary Wilson, was baptised. It was a nice thought of William's to give his first-born daughter the same name as his mother had. John Woodale the mariner from Whitehaven was related by marriage to these Wilsons, and in his will of 1730 remembered a number of them with small bequests.

The Browns, William and 'Elinor' again, also lived at Greaves Ground at this time, presumably the one family in the newer farmhouse and the other in the older dwelling that had come to be considered rather as a subsidiary cottage. William Brown had two children, John, baptised in 1712 who died in infancy, and Jane, baptised in 1713. He had books in his home, valued at five shillings on his death at the age of 32 in 1714. Possibly this represents quite a number. When Thomas Atkinson's estate at Hoathwaite had been apprized in 1688, 'two bibles and other books' were valued at only tenpence. The same valuation was placed on 'one swine and poultry' on the next line, as if the prizers had got down to the odds and ends by this stage. Jane Brown remained at Greaves Ground for many years, and in 1733 she was married from there to Matthew Redhead of Heathwaite Yate, Kirkby in Furness, a place situated on the Duddon estuary beyond Broughton, about 10 miles away by modern roads, but less by the old way which led into the Woodland valley from Greaves Ground, by Haverigg Holme and Climb Stile.

What, however, are we to make of the Barkers? This family must also have been at Greaves Ground for a fair portion of the same period – Richard and yet another Eleanor (they practised a wonderful liberality in their spelling!) whose children, Elizabeth, Thomas and Eleanor, were baptised in 1715, 1716 and 1722 respectively. Wherever did they all put themselves? At least the married Wilson boy, Willyam, moved to nearby Rose Hill soon after the birth of his daughter Elianor, because he was living there in 1723 when his son Isaac was baptised. This Willyam carried on his father's tradition of public service, becoming churchwarden in 1751.

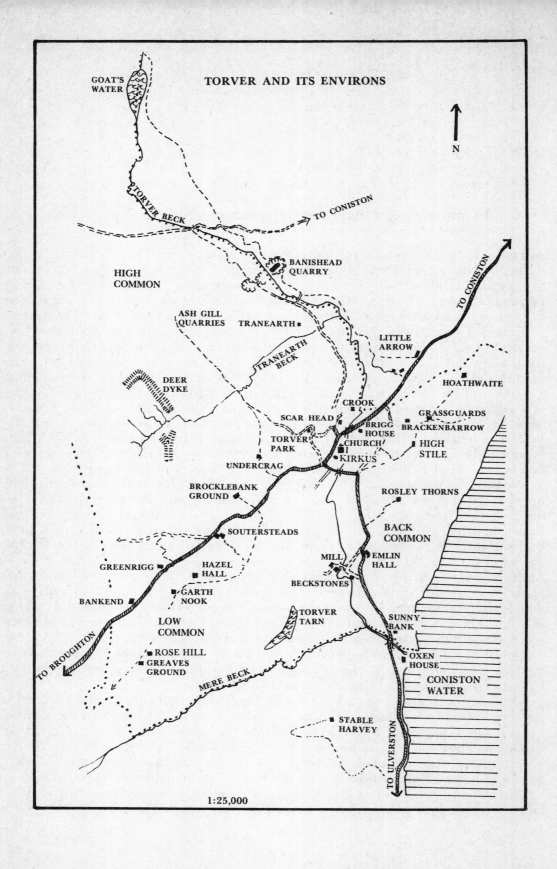

TORVER AND ITS ENVIRONS

N

GOAT'S WATER

TORVER BECK

TO CONISTON

HIGH COMMON

BANISHEAD QUARRY

TO CONISTON

ASH GILL QUARRIES

TRANEARTH

LITTLE ARROW

HOATHWAITE

TRANEARTH BECK

DEER DYKE

CROOK

SCAR HEAD

GRASSGUARDS

BRIGG HOUSE

BRACKENBARROW

TORVER PARK

CHURCH

HIGH STILE

UNDERCRAG

KIRKUS

BROCKLEBANK GROUND

ROSLEY THORNS

BACK COMMON

SOUTERSTEADS

GREENRIGG

HAZEL HALL

MILL

EMLIN HALL

BANKEND

GARTH NOOK

BECKSTONES

LOW COMMON

TORVER TARN

SUNNY BANK

TO BROUGHTON

ROSE HILL
GREAVES GROUND

OXEN HOUSE

MERE BECK

CONISTON WATER

STABLE HARVEY

TO ULVERSTON

1:25,000

Just along the road into the village from Greaves Ground, at Hazel Hall, there seems to have been less congestion. This was the home of Daniel and Margaret Fleming, whose son William was baptised in 1718. Later, William Jackson and family replaced these Flemings, and the impression from the registers is of an indifferently thriving community. In 1737 Sarah, the daughter, died, and two years later William also lost his wife, Bridget. Garth Nook, which stands in roughly the same relationship to Hazel Hall as Rose Hill to Greaves Ground, and is now a roofless ruin, beautifully situated with a commanding prospect over the upper part of the Woodland Valley, an overgrown garden on its eastern side, was the home of Edward and Annas Atkinson. Their son John was baptised in 1706. Edward was a member of the Court Baron jury and 'cunstabal' in 1715. By 1719, however, George Wilson, a tailor, was living there. Within living memory (1980) the tailor used to visit the separate homesteads of the valley, just as George must have done. His wife's name is not given, but his sons, John, William and Jonathan, are recorded in 1719, 1722 and 1724. George himself died in 1735.

From Hazel Hall more than one trackway crosses the moor or heathland to other parts of the parish, leading to peat mosses or near old bloomery sites on the Low Common. This common is more open and desolate now than it would have been in the early 18th century, when, for example, we might have encountered William Wilson or William Jackson leading peat down the track, or getting brackens for winter bedding. We could follow one of these ways over the rocky hill pasture towards Moor, an aptly named farm on the edge of the cultivable land. Here again there lived at least two families. William Atkinson, yeoman, and his wife Sarah raised a considerable family at Moor; Isabel, baptised 1715, Thomas 1716, Sarah 1718, William 1720, and Agnes 1724. At least as early as 1718 there was also John Fleming, yeoman, whose son Miles was baptised in that year. But there is no further reference to him, and in 1719 John, son of John Brocklebank, yeoman, and his wife Annis (another variant of Agnes) was baptised, followed in 1724 by William. There seems to be no consistent principle determining whether a person should be described as 'yeoman'. Private inclination perhaps had as much to do with it as anything, or a desire to give a small boost to one's status. Anyone trying to farm the marginal land around Moor would need all the boost they could get and, even allowing for the high mortality rate of those days, one wonders how all these folk made a living, even how they managed to find enough to eat. Perhaps they didn't. In 1716 the Manor Court fined William Crowdson of the Moor one shilling for encroaching on the common – the same treatment which had been meted out to William Atkinson for this offence in the previous year.

A good road winds from below Moor across to Park Ground. Like Moor, this is not one of the oldest settlements in Torver. Its name suggests that it was enclosed from the 'waste', possibly as late as the early 16th century. As might be expected, the principal family here was the Parkes. The tradition of linking the name of a family with its place of residence was quite common in the 16th century: another Torver example, from 1599, is 'John of the More'. In 1702 Edward and Elizabeth Parke celebrated the baptism of their son 'Willyam', and there were Parkes at Parke throughout the period – James, another son, was churchwarden in 1733, and Elizabeth died in 1741. Robert Parke, of Parke Ground, described as 'wright', and his son Leonard had done most of the building work at Sir Daniel Fleming's new forge at

Coniston in 1675, for which they received altogether £48 6s. 8d. Meanwhile, there had been a branch of the Atkinson clan (William) in residence at Parke as late as 1711. Presumably they had gone across to Moor soon after this, and had been succeeded by the Cassons, Thomas and Mary, whose son James was baptised in 1720. In that year too there was baptised from Parke, Hannah, the daughter of Anthony High, yeoman. This title was almost certainly a hopeful gesture to magnify Anthony's status. He and his family moved from place to place, probably always inhabiting the least desirable cottage on the farmstead; they turn up at Undercrag in 1725 and at Scarhead in 1735. The Cassons were certainly still at Park Ground in 1724, when their daughter Dinah was baptised.

Beyond Parke the road continues down below ancient hedges which may well have been planted by these Parkes and Cassons, through small green pastures to the river just above the mill. The building has been converted into a private house, and little remains to indicate its former industrial usage. Jno. Atkinson was living at the nearby mill house in 1714. He had been overseer of the poor in 1701 when Mary Brockbank signed a receipt for five shillings, 'in full of all demands till this time by me'; Atkinsons had been actively, not to say notoriously and nefariously, associated with the mill in Elizabethan times. But the milner who died in 1718 was Jno. Biggins whose children, William and Agnes, were baptised in 1716 and 1718 respectively. Whether accident or sickness carried him off we do not know, nor what happened to his young family. Later deaths recorded at the mill are James Bigland who was described as the milner, in 1739, and Joseph Askew in 1741.

Bigland placed himself a rung above all these yeomen in the social hierarchy: 'Gentleman' is the term used in the inventory of his 'goods, cattels and chattels' which was apprized not, as was usual, by two or three of the other Torver folk, but by James Taylor of Appletreeholm, Blawith, and Benjamin Taylor of Nibthwaite Town, both places several miles down the Crake valley. The scale of his possessions goes some way to justifying his social pretensions. He had two silver cups and three spoons, valued together at £5, and each of which was itemised in his will. Included in the contents of the 'middle room' (an amenity that none of his neighbours possessed) were six chairs and a looking glass. In the 'parlour' was a chest of drawers. The valuation of £1 10s. for the 'wooden vessel, and one iron girdle, brandreth, one iron pan, with all other iron vessels belonging to the house' was higher than the corresponding entry in any other inventory. By bequeathing his specialist milner's equipment to James, his eldest son, he clearly expected the business to stay in the family. In addition to his interest in the mill, he had a stake in the land, like everyone else, leaving behind 'six beasts, old and young' (value £11), 'one old mare' (5s.) and 42 indifferent sheep (£5 the lot), as well as stocks of hay and straw, bigg (barley), oats, meal and malt. Specific references to peats and fuel for the house is a vivid reminder of the degree of self-sufficiency which was forced on these remote country dwellers.

Naturally, the mill was a focal point of the community, and roads led away in all directions. One ran straight to nearby Beckstones. This is a classic example of the small upland farmstead, sheltered by the hillside from the worst of the weather, and facing slightly east of south, its inbye land (fields nearest the house) sloping away to the rushing tree-lined beck. John and Mary Park lived here with their family – Susannah, baptised in 1715, John in 1720 and James in 1724. It must have been a dreadful blow to Mary when John, 'husbandman' of Beckstones, died later that year, leaving his stock and a bare minimum of equipment to sustain the stricken family. His beasts were valued at £8, as were his sheep. Using the Bigland inventory as a guide, this would mean four cattle and upwards of 60 sheep. His household goods and husbandry gear together were valued at no more than Bigland's iron pans and vessels.

Another road from the mill led over the Low Common to Stable Harvey, although this is by no means obvious today. Stable Harvey, one of the oldest settlements in the area, remains an isolated little kingdom, guarding its independence by the slopes and heathlands which surround it. There must have been several dwellings in the early 18th century, and for many years a school was conducted in what is now one of the farm outbuildings. A. P. Brydson, writing in the early years of the 20th century, commented that 'up to quite recent years there was a school at Stable Harvey, kept by an elderly woman, at which many of the youth of the neighbourhood were educated. This lady, Mrs. Mawson, afterwards went to Langdale, where she gave instruction in spinning and weaving in the School of Art established there for the encouragement of local industries.' John Brocklebank, weaver, brought his bride, Susan Park of Beckstones (John Park's sister) to Stable Harvey from Em Hall in 1719, a year after their marriage when a son, John, was born to them, followed in 1721 and 1724 by Thomas and William. Susan, a daughter born in 1729, was to marry John Tennant in 1761. He was 'a miner in the parish of Clanroughan in the County of Carnarvon in Wales', who had surely been attracted to the Lake District by the prospect of work in its extractive industries. Social mobility in the 18th century was greater than one might expect.

John Brocklebank the father died in 1741, leaving cattle worth only £6, and household stuff and husbandry gear at a miserable 15 shillings. In the same year Joseph Parke also died. This branch of the Parke family had been at Stable Harvey for many years. In 1703 Edward had married 'Eliner' Wilson of Undercragg, 'with a Nonconformist priest'. This is a slightly sinister note, in keeping with both the independence of Stable Harvey and with the note, dated 1717, in the church records, that, although John Stope was a careful and diligent minister, who administered the Lord's supper twice yearly, there were in the chapelry both Presbyterians and Anabaptists. Other identifiable Stable Harvey families include Taylors – in 1701 Richard son of James and 'Issabel', was baptised – and Lows. Richard Low, husbandman, died in 1738, and soon afterwards, John, son of widow Low. Neither family makes any great impact on the parish records; they were of the kind that maintain the state of the world, and have left no memorial. However, by comparison with his neighbour John Brocklebank, Richard must have lived quite comfortably – the (unspecified) goods in his fire room, the principal living apartment, for example, were worth £1 10s.

On a more positive note, in 1735 Dorothy Parke had married Luke Brown of Oxenhouse, the next farmhouse in this circuit of Torver, reached from Stable Harvey over pleasantly-sloping pasture land divided by hawthorn hedges and punctuated by great trees. This was land which Richard Low might easily have worked, the trees after all a lasting memorial. Oxenhouse is situated by the lake shore on the south side of the mouth of Torver beck, technically in the parish of Blawith. It was occupied by Browns and Parkes, large families both. In the year after Luke's wedding, Hannah

Brown married William Birkett of Crook, a short-lived marriage as she died in 1740. Luke and Hannah were children of the Nicholas Brown who in 1715 died untimely, like John Park of Beckstones. Nicholas was one of the middling sort of husbandmen. He must have had six or seven beasts (valuation £12 10s. 6d.), getting on for a hundred sheep (£12) and he kept bees. Moreover 15 separate sums of money were owing to him, ranging from £1 to £13, amounting in all to £55 9s. 9d. One of his debtors was his neighbour, poor John Park, who had borrowed £2 10s., presumably to enable him to set up house with his bride at Beckstones. The other identifiable borrowers came from as far afield as Oxen Park on the road out to the Rusland valley from Ulverston, in one direction, and Grasmere in the other.

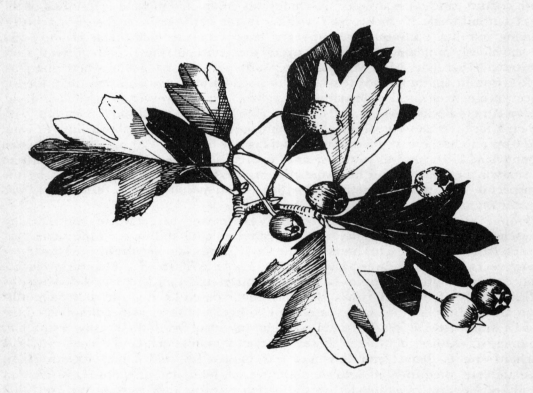

At the time of Nicholas's death, Thomas and Annis Park were establishing their family at Oxenhouse. In 1719 they had a mass baptism of the children who had accumulated to date: Joel (who took up basket making and was later to move to Whitehaven), Tamar, John, Thomas and Agnes. When Mary arrived in 1721 and Jonas in 1724, they were baptised in the usual way. Thomas himself died in 1738 at what we would consider only early middle age, as did many of the men who figure in this chronicle. But then, it must have told on him, coping with a family of that size, in the living conditions of the time. Just across the river from Oxenhouse is Sunny Bank, then the home of Richard Parke, churchwarden in 1716, whose daughter Mary married Thomas Birkett of Crook in 1733 at the age of nineteen. In 1739 Thomas was included as one of the assessors to the Court Baron.

From Sunny Bank the modern road winds up the hill passing Beckstones on the left, to Em, Elm or Emlin Hall at the top. William Brocklebank lived here at the beginning of the period. His children were Agnes, 1713, and Thomas, 1715. John Brocklebank, probably William's younger brother, has already been mentioned. Later, in 1727, Edward son of Thomas Mather, milner, was baptised. The connection with the mill continued, because after James Bigland the miller died in 1739, his widow Ruth was at Elm How, where she died in 1742. Elizabeth Wilson lived here also, and in 1722 she was baptised, being of adult age. Six years later she married Anthony Benson, clothier, whose address is again Elm How, and whose first wife, also an Elizabeth, had died in 1721. Anthony himself lived until 1745.

Hidden away in a fold of the ground behind Elm How on the edge of the Back Common is Rosley Thorns, a place which has very little recorded history, possibly because even if you live in Torver, you may be totally unaware of its existence. In the early 18th century Parks and Wilsons lived there. Edward Park was churchwarden in 1707, had a son by his wife 'Elianor', John by name, in 1723, and in 1746 was churchwarden again. This chronology argues a greater longevity than the normal, and an early introduction to public responsibility. But in 1714 Richard Parke of Stable Harvey had died at the age of 77; and Joel Park of Oxenhouse was churchwarden at the age of 31 in 1738, the same year that his father died. The only information about James Wilson of Rosley Thorns is that on his death in 1733 he was described as 'yeoman'. Then in 1748 Elizabeth Chamley, 'widow and boarder at Rosley Thorns', died. This kind of entry in the register is not uncommon. In 1709 Alice Lees, an 'old woeman', died at Oxenhouse, and in 1734 at Emlin Hall, Elizabeth Taylor 'a poor woman belonging to Nibthwaite'.

Dropping back to the main road over the field where one can still see the marks of old ploughing, and passing the site of the village pound, one soon reaches Hollace – Hollow House. Robert Jenkinson died here in 1721. He may well have been one of the Jenkinsons later associated with Stable Harvey; William Jenkinson 'taylor', and his wife 'Cathrine', had two sons, the elder, Robert, baptised in 1732 and William, in 1735. There were also Wilsons, William and Alice, whose daughter Agnes was baptised in 1719. The Garners, Ephraim, Ruth and their four children, also lived here. Along with William Fleming, Ephraim was given a considerable responsibility by the Manor Court in 1738. It was to check that no one put into Torver meadows (the town fields) more than their proper stint, ie. for every half acre, one beast. James, eldest of the Garner children, was to be churchwarden in 1751, two years after his father's death.

The real Wilson stronghold is a little farther along the road, reached by a long drive, High Stile, fully meriting its name as it looks over the vale to the fells beyond. A stone inserted in the front wall of the farmhouse is dated 1720, and commemorates William and Margaret Wilson. They had three children, Thomas 1716, John 1718 and Jane 1723, the same year as William took his turn as churchwarden. In 1715 he had been one of the assessors for the Court Baron jury, as young Thomas was to be in 1739. Like the Parkes and the Atkinsons, the Wilsons were to be found in several places at this time. The other William Wilson, from Hollace, moved to Grassguards soon after 1719. Grassguards is now a romantically situated ruin on the edge of the back common, north of High Stile on the road leading beyond Brackenbarrow to the woodland above the lake. In the tiny farmhouse and tinier cottage lived the Harrisons as well as the Wilsons. The register entries respecting both families make sad reading.

In 1738 Thomas Harrison married Ann Walker, both of Grassguards, and their son Thomas was baptised in 1741. But Ann was his second wife; in 1737 little Elizabeth Harrison had been buried on 19 April, and Elizabeth, wife of Thomas Harrison, on 3 August. Life treated William Wilson more unkindly still. He was enabled to make no second start. For the years 1722, 1723 and 1724 the registers record the burial of stillborn children to William and Alice Wilson. In 1724 Jane Wilson, 'widow and pauper', died. Almost certainly she was William's mother, and the word 'pauper' strikes a chill note. Alice Wilson lived until 1747; William himself for another 10 years, and the last entry reads, 'a poor man'. Not that he would be alone during those last years. A whole cast of supporting characters moves in and out of Grassguards: Flemings to begin with – David, whose son Daniel was baptised in 1716, and Myles whose daughter Mary died at the age of 22 in 1719, the same year as his wife, Margaret. Agnes Chamley had died in 1709, and an earlier Elizabeth Harrison in 1712, so the Harrisons at any rate were not fugitive occupants. Yet one wonders where Ann Walker had been putting herself before she married Thomas Harrison. And wherever did James Pritt, who died in 1742, do his weaving? How indeed did he live? His inventory is so brief as to be cursory – 15s. 6d. for his entire effects, whilst the comparatively enormous sum of £188 15s. 4d. is recorded as owing to him 'on specialty', ie. under sealed contract. Also included in the deaths for 1742 was Elizabeth Fleming, widow, most likely the relict of David. It was she who wished to contribute to the Torver charities on a very modest scale. One may feel the modesty rather overdone, because although her effects were valued at only 10 shillings, she had £70 lent out upon specialty. It begins to look as if the squalid little hovels of Grassguards may have housed a nest of moneylenders. However, by 1753 Thomas and Elizabeth Wilkinson had arrived. In this year their daughter Martha was baptised, and we may hope that she cheered William Wilson's last years a little.

The atmosphere around Brackenbarrow, not many yards to the west, but, like High Stile overlooking the main valley, is as open and cheerful as the ambience of Grassguards is claustrophobic and doom-laden. Jacksons lived here throughout the period, most notably John, 'yeoman' again but with more justification than most, who was churchwarden in 1742. John and his wife Mary had six children between 1729 and 1740, but two of the boys died before their fifth year. In the early part of the century a family of Perkins lived and worked somewhere at Brackenbarrow. John who was buried in 1711 had been a shoemaker, as was Francis, one of the Oxenhouse Browns, who died in 1726. There were also Wilsons about the place. William, 'of Brakanbaray', was appointed 'heglokear' (hedge-looker) in 1715, the same year as his daughter Elizabeth was baptised. It seems as though William and Mary Fleming arrived when the Wilsons left. Their daughter Mary was baptised in 1719. By the next year they had moved to Scar Head, leaving their house at Brackenbarrow to be occupied by Daniel and Margaret Fleming, whose daughter, yet another Elizabeth, was baptised soon after they took up residence. This family remained for the rest of the period. Mary the second daughter, who was born in 1723, lived until 1739, the year in which John Jackson was acting as constable. Yet somewhere, in the midst of all these permanent Jacksons and Flemings, Dorothy, daughter of Christopher and

Agnes Stephenson, was baptised in 1734, and in 1742 Mary Pool, 'old woman and boarder', died.

Continuing north along the flattened ridge from Brackenbarrow, a now largely disused cartway leads to Hoathwaite, where John and Mary Atkinson lived. He was a tanner by trade. One of his sons, Thomas, died in 1723 at the age of seventeen. His daughter Mary married George Eskrigg of Overkellett (near Carnforth in Lancashire) in 1724 when she was 20, a contrast to the more usual practice of marrying within the local community. Another son, Isaac, also a tanner, followed the commoner arrangement by marrying in 1735 Dinah Wennington of Lind End, Broughton Mills (the adjacent parish on the southerly side of Torver). Then, having lost her within months of their wedding, he married in 1739 Lucy Harrison of Church House, by whom he had at least five children. Meanwhile John Atkinson's remaining son, another John, must have stayed at Hoathwaite, because his wife Mary was buried from there in 1756. John the elder had died in 1726, and his Mary five years later. These Atkinsons were better off than most of the Torver families. John's household furniture included table, form, chairs and dresser; also a clock and case, valued at 15 shillings. In 1751 James Brockbank carved his name on one of the big pieces of sandstone that had been used in the construction of the principal barn. He worked at Hoathwaite, if the later, similar inscription of 1862 by John Danson is any guide. The 1851 census records Danson as an agricultural labourer, living at Scar Head.

Church House, where Lucy came from, was basically another Fleming stronghold. Margaret died in 1737, followed in the next year by her husband, John. He had been the village blacksmith, so that an anvil is listed among his effects, incongruously mentioned with a stone of wool and valued at £1 1s. Agnes who had married John Atkinson of Souterstead in 1732 was their daughter, and William Fleming, appointed pinder in 1739, a son. Also in this open, low-lying area in the centre of the vale was Brigg House, situated next to the bridge by which the road from Coniston crosses Torver beck. More Jacksons lived here; John again, but this one married to an Eleanor. His daughter Mary, baptised in 1720, married in 1741 Ismael Wennington of Undercrag, who figures largely in this period as witness to wills and inventories. The Elizabeth Jackson described by the apprizers of her effects as 'Widow Jackson', who died in 1738, would be John's mother, and the Elizabeth who died in 1739 an unmarried sister. The duplication of names must have been a trial even to the people at the time!

Continuing up-river from the bridge we pass by Crook, very properly situated on rather higher ground in a bend of the stream. Although Leonard Parke was here in 1703, later references are all to the family of Thomas and Annis Birkett. Their children were Thomas 1708, Daniel 1709, William 1712, Elizabeth 1716 and John 1719. Thomas the elder is another 'yeoman', and in 1723 he was churchwarden. William married Hannah Brown from Oxenhouse and in 1748 he too took his turn as churchwarden. John and his mother both died in 1740, 10 years before Thomas himself. Understandably, the inventory of young John's chattels is a brief one: work tools (but what manner of work?) 5s. 6d., an old watch (had it been his grandfather's?) 10s. 6d. If only John and William Jackson, the apprizers, had been more specific: but of course, they knew what John's work had been, and no doubt, all about his watch, so there was no need to go into detail.

In this part of Torver there is a wonderful complexity of stone-walled roads, and the one which passes Crook winds round past a cottage, said to have been used as the parsonage at one time, to Scar Head. Today the remains of the farm are relatively scanty, but in the early 18th century there was a remarkable profusion of names, suggesting a number of cottages rather than one smallholding. In 1705 Daniel, son of Myles and Dorothy Fleming, was baptised; Daniel does not reappear in the Scar Head records, but his brother Robert figures in a most melancholy catalogue of misfortune. In 1725, the year his mother died, he married Margaret Rownson of Scarhead (perhaps a farm servant, who had been indentured as an apprentice in her early teens), but in 1726 she died four days after the delivery of a stillborn son. Maybe his sorrows made Robert reckless, for the inventory of his goods when he died in 1730 leaves a mere eightpence credit balance after allowing for all debts and funeral expenses. Maybe he did a bit of cattle dealing, for he had an unusually large number of animals – horses at £3 6s. 8d. (at least three or four of them), about a hundred sheep at £12 in value, and a herd of heifers, cows and steers, £30. Another possibility is that he had been involved in tanning, because another thing he left behind was oak bark worth £1 6s. 8d. Myles Fleming the father died the year after his son. We may picture Myles as a 'typical' farmer. His household equipment was adequate, but unspectacular. His principal resource was his livestock – a horse, cows and other beasts valued at £15 10s., so they probably numbered eight or nine, and sheep, £25 6s. 8d., a figure representing probably about two hundred animals. By the will they all went to his son William, leaving Thomas, the other surviving son, with only half a crown in money.

William Fleming and his wife Mary appear regularly in the Scar Head records after 1731, having now taken over from Myles. Although they lost an infant son, David, in 1738, they managed to raise a family of five children during this decade. William was Court Baron assessor in 1739 and churchwarden in 1754, a position which Myles had held as long ago as 1706. Clearly there were Flemings at Scar Head throughout the period. But numbers of other folk appear, often briefly, in the registers. Roger Whinfield married Agnes Swinburne in 1723. Both were of Scar Head. Two years later Frances Swinburne, Agnes's sister we may suppose, married William Swainson of Torver Park. Then in 1726 Jane Leck married Michael Atkinson of Coniston Hall. Did Myles Fleming happen to have a particularly attractive series of servant girls at this time? In between all these weddings, in 1725, Edward Jackson, husbandman, died. He was more literate than many of his neighbours – in 1712 he had composed and written out a will for old Mary Atkinson at Undercrag, and his belongings included books, worth 3s. 4d. Tantalisingly, no further detail is given.

The number of separate cottages in this part of the village gives the clue to the multiplicity of non-Fleming names at Scar Head, and also to the apparent confusion between addresses. The Whinfield family illustrates how in this part of the parish one place ran into the next. At the time everyone knew exactly where everyone else lived but, after two and a half centuries, the Whinfields are exceedingly difficult to disentangle. Christian names offer the best clue. From at least Commonwealth times until the late 1720s when they moved to Park Ground, Roger Whinfields lived at Scar Head. One of the girls, Elizabeth, was unusual in that she married Peter Russell of Newcastle, a wine cowper, in 1707. Maybe Peter was in the habit of travelling as far as High Furness in search of suitable wood for his trade. Then the branch of the family which kept to 'William' as the name for the eldest son lived close by, at Torver Park, from before the end of the 17th century; in 1750 the current William was taking his turn as churchwarden. The Whinfields were tanners, and persons of some consequence in the parish, if we may judge by the large number of inventories that William, 'Sen<sup>r</sup>' was asked to apprize.

A contrasting person at Scar Head was Anthony High whom we met at Park in 1720. He had migrated across the valley by the mid-1720s, and it was whilst at Scar Head that he and Dorothy added to their family responsibilities in 1726, when Dinah was born, followed by Daniel (in compliment to the Flemings, perhaps) in 1731, Sarah (who died in infancy) in 1733 and Anthony in 1736. He must have continued his nomadic existence for the whole of his life, for it was in nearby Woodland that Anthony Hye, 'a poor man', died in 1743. One can only hope that it was possible to find somewhere for Dorothy and the children to go. Robert Airey may have been Anthony's successor as hired man at Scar Head. His son John died in 1745. He could not have stayed long, however, for there are no more Airey entries, and in 1748 John Briggs of Scar Head, another 'poor man', died. It begins to look as if William Fleming had been as unlucky in his hinds as Myles had been fortunate in his girls; but a period of greater stability followed when Enoch and Dorothy Atkinson arrived, and at intervals throughout the 1750s their children were baptised.

Moving from Scar Head by the walled road which runs just above what would have been the swamp line, we soon come to Torver Park, and from here a way leads up past High Park through the woods to the High Common. The registers seldom distinguish between High and Low Park, so this settlement must have been regarded as a unit, with the main farmhouse almost certainly on the site of the house now known as High Park. At Low Park is the ruin of the *Pack Saddle* inn and a number of cottages. This was the most thickly populated part of Torver. Flemings, again, were present for the entire half century, but it is almost impossible to work out a coherent picture of their family relationships. William Fleming, whose wife Dorothy died in 1727, was a butcher. Agnes who died in 1726 was described as 'widow and pauper'. Thomas Fleming married Mary Brown, also of Torver Park, in 1737, and died in 1741. It looks as if Benjamin Lyon who came in the early 1720s must have married one of the Fleming girls, because he christened his firstborn son 'Fleming'. Then the deaths of three of his children are recorded during the 1730s. Thomas could well have been the son to whom Myles Fleming of Scar Head bequeathed 2s. 6d. If so, Myles had possibly figured that he was less in need than his brother William. His inventory reveals a comfortably furnished home – cupboards, tables, dressers, chairs and stools, – and a modicum of culture – books at 3s. 4d. again (one wonders whether the apprizers always put down 3s. 4d. or 6s. 8d. because they had no idea how much books were really worth, and they didn't care much for such things themselves). He also had an adequately stocked farm, with kine valued at £16 and sheep at £12. Sundry debtors owed him just over £50, including an item for £10, being 'money owing to the deceased upon a bargen'. He himself left debts amounting to £15 15s., one of which was £5 owing 'upon bill to Eliz. Fleming, Grassguards'.

Another of these narrow-walled cartways leads from Torver Park to the church. It is known as Car Lane, from the swampy nature of the ground that it crosses. Near the church are two old houses, Wilson Cottages and the Smithy, but neither of them is referred to by name in the 18th-century registers. John Fleming who lived just across the way at Church House was described as 'Smith' in 1727. There had been Flemings here from at least the time of James II, as well as a branch of the Parkes, whose association with the house certainly dates back to 1617 when a son of Leonard Parke was baptised. However, the last specific Parke reference is for 1714, and thereafter the Flemings were in sole possession. John, who had been churchwarden in 1714 when Elizabeth Parke was buried, lived until 1738, a year after the death of his wife Margaret. His son William was appointed pinder in 1739. Further descendants, mostly Johns or Williams, were still there when the French Revolution broke out.

Returning along Car Lane to Low Park, we may bear left through fields and over stiles to Undercrag, where, as at Hoathwaite and High Stile, a new house was built in the 18th century. 'Willyam' and Mary Wilson lived here at the beginning of the period. Their daughter Mary was baptised in 1702, and their son Thomas in 1708. In 1722 Dorothy, another daughter, married John Leech, also of Undercrag. Their family is remarkable for the length of time that separates the baptisms of their children: 1725 Sarah, 1732 Mary, 1739 another Dorothy. Poor little Thomas Wilson survived only until 1711, and Willyam himself died in 1727. His occupation was, unusually, slater. In those days the quarries were worked on a small scale for the local market only, so that being a slater was not a full-time job. Like almost everyone else, Willyam kept some livestock: beasts, worth £2 10s., and sheep, £1. This represents no more than six or eight sheep, and two house cows, one in milk and the other dry, in calf. He also had part of a hive of bees worth 2s. 6d., a difficult thing to share, one would imagine. The list of miscellaneous goods includes 'baggs and a sack, 2s. 0d.', the kind of detail that would have been welcome as relating to book titles or individual kitchen utensils. William and Mary Fleming were here in 1727, en route for Scar Head from Brackenbarrow, when their daughter Elizabeth was baptised. Then in the 1730s we meet Robert and Agnes Fleming, whose sons John and William were baptised in 1736 and 1738. Robert was a saddletree maker; he had brought Agnes as his bride from Bleansley in Broughton Mills in 1735.

The mid-1720s was a busy time for weddings in Torver. Two took place from Undercrag as well as the Scar Head ones: John Mawson and Elizabeth Dixon, both of Undercrag, in 1724, and in 1725 Timothy Hartley, house carpenter, and Isabell Braithwaite, both of Undercrag. Not one of this quartet figures further in the records. Perhaps they moved away. There were certainly plenty of other, apparently unrelated, people about, Michael and Margaret Smith, for example, who had been at Torver Park in 1721, but whose second son, James, was baptised from Undercrag in 1723. Occasionally one is tempted to think that the clerk must have been careless. In 1728 John, son of John and Dorothy Leech, was baptised from Torver Park. Yet at this time they 'ought' to have been at Undercrag, with long gaps between the births of their children. Could it be that John Leech had hired himself out to a different master for that year, and then returned to the devil he knew? Back in Undercrag, in 1725 the peripatetic Anthony High pops up again, this time alas as the father of a stillborn son. In 1724 Agnes, daughter of David and Agnes Fleming, died. The Flemings hereabouts bring to mind, rather irreverently, the Flopsy Bunnies. There are such confusing numbers of them!

David Fleming, saddletree maker, died in 1731. In addition to the usual small tally of animals and the usual unquantified reference to arable crops – 'bigg, oats and other grain' – he had owned 'a little mare' and a Bible. In the list of his debtors is

Anthony High, for 12 shillings, as well as folk for whom he had done work in all parts of Cumberland – Keswick, Wigton and Bootle. The person from Bootle was no less than Samuel Towers, whose will was to figure largely in the chronicle of Torver charities. The feeling comes through from this inventory that David was a nice man, willing to put himself out for other people, and for whom, in turn, the apprizers were prepared to do a detailed, painstaking job. Then David Fleming, cordwainer, died in 1735 and Ann Fleming in 1739. To add a little interest in the way of variety, Dorothy Jackson, spinster, had died at Undercrag in 1714. She may well have been sister to Edward, over at Scar Head, and lived at Undercrag as a long-serving farm servant.

The Thomas Brocklebank who died in 1741 seems to have been quite unconnected with anyone else of the same name. Unusually, he had no stake in the land whatever, but money owing to him 'upon bills and bonds and other security, and without security' amounted to £35 15s. – not a person one could take to, in the way that David Fleming was. Other Undercraggians in the early part of the period were John Atkinson, householder, and Mary Atkinson, formerly of Ulverston. If we may judge by her will, Mary had been something of a character. Having bequeathed £8 to Mary Russell of Backbarrow, her granddaughter, she left one shilling to each of her natural[1] sons, Roger Atkinson and Benjamin Atkinson. Also to receive a shilling, but without any specific reference to a relationship with Mary, were George Towers of Yewdale (in Coniston) and Agnes Atkinson of Undercrag. Later we meet Ishmael Wennington again, when he brought his bride here in 1741, and whose daughter Elizabeth was baptised in the same year. The beginning of the Parke connexion with Undercrag may be detected in 1751 when Fleming, son of Leonard and 'Joice' Parke was born.

Beyond Undercrag and almost cowering below the steep hillside is Brocklebank Ground, much less fully documented and, until the Parkes built the new houses soon after the middle of the century, probably consisting of only a pair of tiny cottages, Grassguards style. A Brocklebank did live here in the early 18th century, Thomas, who was churchwarden in 1717 and whose wife Jane died in 1719. He was fined by the Manor Court in 1715 for encroaching upon the common, and for turning water out of its ancient course at the lower side of Roger Fleming's wood. Clearly he was a man who did not allow the sacred and the secular spheres to get too much intermingled. He may be the same man whose death at Undercrag is recorded in 1741. In the second cottage were the Bensons; Benjamin, son of the picturesquely named Solomon, was baptised from here in 1718. The Parkes must have arrived before 1734, the year in which Edward was churchwarden, but they were not the sole occupants. Margaret Tayler, 'a single woman', died there in 1742. Perhaps she was a boarder. Certainly she was not a poor old woman. Her chattels included two pairs of sheets and a brass pot, and she had £185 owing to her upon specialty.

Farther south again below the road which climbs above the valley floor on its way to Broughton is Souterstead, another of the oldest settlements in Torver. Branches of the Fleming and Atkinson families lived here. Robert Fleming, yeoman, was churchwarden in 1709 and died in 1727. He was another substantial and successful farmer, who had kept a flock of about 200 sheep and six or seven beasts. Like many of the other farmers he had stocks of grain as well as hay in his barn. The importance of his horse to his economy was such that it was placed at the head of the inventory, valued with furniture, at the high figure of £3. Evidence of material prosperity comes not only from the cushions included with the chairs, forms and stools, but also from the presence of a clock worth £2 10s. In 1729 his daughter Elizabeth married Richard Lowther of Broughton. Over the succeeding years Richard had to sustain the deaths of his infant son Robert in 1735, his wife's mother Elizabeth in 1737 and his wife in 1742, as well as his one year old daughter Elizabeth, leaving him to cope with the upbringing of three young sons. By 1747 he had found the help that he must have sorely needed, for on 12 April he married Sarah Parke of Monk Coniston.

The Atkinson family was also closely linked with Greenrigg, a marvellously sited farm overlooking the upper part of the Woodland valley, and across to Greaves Ground where this pilgrimage began. Patriarchal Thomas Atkinson died in 1701, and then there were two Atkinson families; that of William, who was Thomas's executor, and later, that of Michael. William and his wife Tamar had a large number of children, even by the standards of those days. He was a weaver by occupation, took his turn as churchwarden in 1713 and was appointed hedge-looker in 1715. He seems to have lived until 1756, by which time his daughter Jane had married Isaac Wilson of Rose Hill and had two daughters of her own. Michael, who did his stint of hedge-looking in 1739, died the year afterwards. He had what must have been regarded as a sizeable library, for his books were valued at 6s. 8d., twice as much as anyone else's. A family of Brocklebanks also lived here. Hannah, daughter of Henry, was baptised in 1718. In 1736 Jno. Brocklebank married Jennet Brockbank, both of Greenrigg; then in the next year Jno. Brocklebank died. There must have been several dwellings at Greenrigg for throughout the period at least one other family was in residence. Thomas Walker, for example, the carpenter, died there in 1718, and in 1720 his daughter Mary married Matthew Jackson of Stephenson Ground, Broughton Mills. He cannot have been in business in a very big way, for his 'tools and all iron gear' were valued at no more than 6s. 8d. The carpentering must have been an occasional sideline, since he also kept the customary handful of beasts and sheep together with an 'old Mare' which must have been very old for the apprizers to set down a value of 6s. 8d. again. Then in the late 1720s William and Mary Fleming were here when their daughter Sarah was baptised in 1729; it really looks as if William spent a decade as hired man living at various farms before taking over Scar Head. Three years later Isaac, son of Isaac and Margaret Gillbank, was baptised, so this family was weathering the hostile reception that had greeted their arrival. Jumping two decades more, in 1753 William Postlethwaite was churchwarden. Nothing else is discoverable about the Postlethwaites, but at least they make a change from Flemings and Atkinsons.

Down the steep hill, continuing along the Broughton road, we soon reach what is for us the end of the line, Bank End, where we find more and more Atkinsons. In 1716 Edward, householder, died; one shudders to imagine what manner of house. Edward's belongings are baldly summarised – iron gear 1s. 1d., household goods 2s., the lowest figure in the whole of this catalogue of the parish. In 1718 Thomas, a shoemaker, was buried. At the end of the next generation Anthony, a waller, died in 1743, closely followed by the wife of John, not to be confused with John Atkinson of Souterstead, up the road. Anthony had been churchwarden in 1739, when John was a member of the Court Baron jury; John took his turn as churchwarden in 1744. The only explicit reference in the whole period to anyone not named Atkinson is to the burial in 1738 of 'Eliner' Askew, widow, and she may have been born an Atkinson, because another Eleanor Askew is named in Anthony's will as his god-daughter, and beneficiary in the sum of five shillings. She was the wife of Edward Askew of Croft End, a couple of miles along the road to Broughton, who was one of the three trustees whose responsibility it was to see that all the provisions of the will were carried out.

Certain features of this journey through the parish make an obvious contrast with the present day, especially the shorter life-span, and the inter-relationship, not to say in-breeding, of the population. The monotony of Christian names as well as surnames is also striking. But more profound than the differences are the similarities as we see our predecessors going about their daily lives, full of the concerns and opportunities, of the hopes and fears through which we share with them the human condition.

**Note**
Only specific references to places, which enable a person's place of residence to be positively identified, have been used in this survey. Fuller consultation of the Constable's Accounts, and a study of the registers using the given data to establish further certain relationships, would enable the picture to be drawn in even greater detail. In any case, not every known detail has been included in this account – eg. names of children and of occasional residents have sometimes been omitted.

*Chapter Ten*

# Homes and Home Life

If one entered the home of any of these Atkinsons or Wilsons, what could one expect to see? There might well be crossed straws, to keep out witches, on the threshold, or threshwood, just inside the door. It is said that anciently the threshwood consisted of a thick piece of old oak let into the ground and secured in the walls on each side; but since such an arrangement, standing five or six inches above the level of the floor, was very inconvenient, the wood came to be replaced by a stone, even with the entrance. Along the oak partitions, which form the walls of the four foot wide passage which runs the full width of the house from the front door, there are sacks of grain, to be taken either to the mill or the market the following day. A pig carcase hangs by the wall; the ends of sickles protrude from the joists; and on a shelf above the door are all manner of carpentry tools. At the end of this hallan passage, on its right-hand side, is a door, the mell door, giving access to a narrow lobby separated by another wooden partition from the principal living area of the house. This partition, which is carved, and bears the original builder's initials, is known as the heck. In the stout octagonal post at the end of the heck an augur hole has been bored, into which a tuft of cow hair has been pegged. This is for cleaning combs. The room to the left of the hallan is the downhouse, from which the staircase rises, and where the washing and brewing is done. Here also a quantity of elding, material for firing, either wood or peat, is stored. In some of the houses the downhouse doubles as a workshop.

The focal point of the living room is the huge fireplace. On a bright day a person may look up to the sky through the straight flue from the hearth. An oven is built into the thickness of the wall on the side of the fire nearer the heck; it contains stockings and yarn for darning. On the other side of the fireplace is a little wall cupboard, called the locker, with a shelf in it, and here all dry articles, such as salt and spices, are kept. Within the great canopy formed by the side walls which support the chimney hood there is room for the family to sit in the warmth on winter evenings, the women knitting, or spinning wool or flax, and the men perhaps carding wool. It is a 'smoky dome' and in moist weather persons sitting by the fire are subject to the 'hallan drop', a black, sooty deposition from above. The fire burns on a hearth, raised a few inches above the floor, and paved. This is well adapted for peat or wood fires; indeed, the tree roots and ash tops which form a large ingredient of the winter fuel would not burn satisfactorily in a grate. The peats, cut from Low Fell above Hazel Hall, provide heat through regular and vigorous operation of the bellows as much as through their own combustion. (It was said, of course, that wood warmed a person three times: when he cut it, when he sawed it and when he burned it.) A beam runs across the chimney opening, the rannel balk, from which hangs a chain suitable for hanging various culinary vessels. Crooks on the chain can be raised or lowered from link to link.

The furnishings in the living room are solid and utilitarian. The largest and most elaborate piece is the bread cupboard opposite the fireplace, standing the full height of the room, and, like the heck, inscribed with the date of its construction and the initials of its original owner. The different compartments of this chest are the usual depository for oatcakes and other eatables which require to be kept dry and out of the reach of mice. On the plain table, also of oak, are wooden trenchers and piggins. These last are small wooden vessels, like half barrels, with one stave longer than the rest to serve as a handle. There is a wooden settle about six feet long on one side of the fire; its seat is formed into a chest with two or three divisions, in which the housewife keeps such things as thread, buttons or lengths of material. The only other large piece of furniture is the sconce.[1] This is kept along the side of the heck, covered with sheepskins for comfort when sitting on it. Underneath, one night's elding is deposited early each evening. The chairs, chests and bedsteads to be found in the house are also of oak, plain and built to last.

Peeled rushes dipped in hot fat provide a feeble light to supplement that provided by the fire after dusk; there is a candlestick on which to fasten them. This is a light upright pole, fixed in a log of wood, and perforated with a row of holes up one side, in which a piece of iron, bent at right angles, and furnished with a socket for holding tallow candles, and a kind of pincers for the rushes, is moved up or down as convenient. Peelings of the rushes tied together are used as besoms for sweeping the flag floors. The family books are on the sill formed in the thickness of the wall where the small window nearest the fire gives a little extra light. Along with the Bible and a prayer book, there is, let us say, the story of Tom Hickathrift (more familiarly Jack the Giant-killer), the *Garland of the Golden Glove* and Sir William Stanley's *Garland*.

*Tallow candle holder hanging from rafters.*

If one had stayed long, roosting in the spare bed partitioned off in the loft, one would soon have discovered a distinct lack of variety about the food. Breakfast was commonly hasty pudding, and bread and cheese in the afternoon, with beer or milk to drink. The hasty pudding was a species of pottage made from the widely-grown black oats known as haver. The 'bread', or rather oatcakes, made from this grain was called 'clapbread'. The housewife, having mixed oatmeal and water to a paste and added salt, sat on the floor with a backboard on her knees. She laid a piece of the paste on this board and then clapped it with her hands until it expanded into a broad thin cake. The locally-grown barley, bigg, was used principally in making malt, since most families brewed their own ale. Wheaten bread was eaten only on special occasions. Small loaves of it were given to persons invited to funerals, which they were expected to 'take and eat' at home in religious remembrance of the departed. These loaves were known as 'Arvel bread', possibly from the Saxon word 'arfull', meaning 'full of reverence'. Then on Good Friday everyone ate fig-sue, a concoction of ale boiled with wheaten bread and figs, sweetened with sugar. It was considered extremely profane to allow the sacred day to pass without dining, or at least supping, on fig-sue.

In summer there was dairy produce to be had in relative abundance; but they ate few garden vegetables except onions, and savoury herbs to put in broth. Easterledges, otherwise alpine bistort, which grows abundantly below High Park, figured among these herbs. This was the main component of the herb pudding which was regarded as a great delicacy to go with veal in the springtime. The recipe is to mix bistort leaves and groats with a small portion of young nettles, a few blades of chives and whatever else of this nature may be available, and boil them all together in a linen bag with the meat. It must have been very refreshing after the chimney-dried mutton or beef of winter. They kept poultry and geese in pens till about the end of February, but otherwise only the Christmas binge broke the drab monotony of the dark days. Then there was a great baking of pies containing goose, mutton or sweetmeats, and special drinks, such as tea. They would start the day with sweet broth, the stock from the mutton which had been boiled for the mince pies, seasoned with sugar, raisins, currants and cloves; they finished the day with draughts of October ale. A benevolent clergyman, writing early in the 19th century, but looking back to the old days, wrote that 'this sort of winter provisions, and the houses being generally built in low situations, and within a foot or two within the ground, caused agues to be prevalent in spring.'

However, the people had an abundance of warm clothing. Natural wool from the dark-fleeced local sheep, slightly mixed with red and blue, made up into a thick, rough, heavy cloth, very hard-wearing, for coats and waistcoats. Women's outer garments were made from the finer wool woven into a kind of serge. Breeches were of leather, usually buckskin. Shirts (sarks) were of harden cloth, of the finest part of the hemp, or the coarsest part of the flax. This harden was exceedingly rough to wear. People used to take the cloth to a battling stone, one that was large, with a smooth and sloping surface, in a convenient beck. Here they would steep the cloth, fold it upon the stone, and beat it with a battling wood. A near contemporary recorded: 'It is surprising how soft the cloth was rendered by a few operations of this nature.' Clogs were the general footwear for both sexes, young and old. Itinerant craftsmen were responsible for making many of these articles of clothing, along with other things needed at the farm – for example, there were hacklers who combed out flax or hemp, and ropers. We know that there were carpenters, shoemakers and tailors in Torver itself at various times. The tailor would make up the cloth at a person's own fireside, no doubt simultaneously acting as a clearing house for local news and gossip. In the mid-18th century he made women's gowns, petticoats and stays as well as men's garments, on account of their being made of much stronger material than became usual in the next century.

The custom in winter was for neighbours to gather in each other's houses, the women spinning as they talked. ' "Ganging a rocking", or going with the rock (distaff) and spindle to the neighbours' houses', wrote J. Briggs in 1822, 'was a favourite pastime among our grandmothers, who had not the most distant idea of the more elegant employment of tea drinking, which has now entirely superseded spinning and knitting.'

If old tradition is a reliable guide, their talk round the fireside often concerned itself with the supernatural, with dobbies, perhaps. These were spirits or ghosts which appeared during the hours of darkness, seldom (conveniently) to more than one person at a time. A dobbie stone, one with a natural hole through it, hung over the door was a sure way of diverting the attention of these characters. Witches were still linked with solitary old women of cross temper and unattractive appearance. They had no power over anything with a cross on it, so butter was printed with a cross. A rowan branch checked their power, so a rowan was often planted (and is still planted) by the farm or house doorway. The kind of tricks to be expected from witches were to make cows cast their calves, to overturn carts of hay or to mislead hunters by turning themselves into a hare. A deeper unease was stirred by wise men, or conjurors, who were supposed to have made a compact with the devil, as Faust did. These wise men were such as had spent their lives in the pursuit of science, and had learned too much. They possessed wonderful power; for example, a wise man could restore stolen goods, either by fetching back the articles, showing the thief in a black mirror, or making him walk round the cross on a market day with the stolen goods on his shoulder. This last he could not do, however, if the culprit wore a piece of green sod upon his head. The wise man was compelled to give the devil some living animal whenever he called upon him, as a pledge that he intended to give himself at last. 'It was usual', wrote Briggs, 'to consider all schoolmasters as wise men, and many an aching heart has the affectionate mother had, lest her darling boy should learn too far.' As the Rev. T. Ellwood was to discover over a century later, these prejudices died hard.

It appears that numbers of ancient customs still flourished in High Furness during the 18th century. Evergreen branches decorated church and homesteads for Christmas, when the day was likely to begin particularly early if a couple of the village men were going the rounds giving a seasonable greeting with voice and fiddle. They would have to be invited in, to take one of the mince pies hanging in a basket over the dairy slab, and to sample the specially brewed 'Christmas drink'. The farmer himself, meanwhile, would be about his work as usual, taking a special sheaf of corn to each of his cows. Later the day was generally celebrated with field sports (the Windermere Harriers still meet in the Coniston/Torver area on Boxing Day), with dancing and card parties.

Marriages were also occasions for general jollification. Everyone in the neighbourhood was 'lated', ie. bidden, to the celebration. There would be a race from the church to the bridal house, when the bride would reward the victor with a ribbon. Then, as the bride sat in splendid state, the guests would accompany their expression of good wishes with money or domestic utensils deposited on her lap. The young men would occupy themselves in races and wrestling before a general dance in a nearby barn brought the day to a triumphant conclusion. Older inhabitants look back nostalgically to such dances to the music of a fiddle, not indeed after weddings, but at the Harvest Home.

The women of the community used to mark a lying-in with some ceremony. Those who had been lated were given frumety (hulled wheat boiled in milk) and sweet butter. The latter was very special. After melting a quantity of butter, the milk was poured off the top. Then the remaining fluid was decanted to leave the salt behind, and mixed into a slurry of rum and sugar already well beaten together with grated nutmeg. Stirred until cool, the resulting ambrosia was the original 'rum butter'. Before going, and as a further mark of the importance of this occasion, the assembled matrons took a dish of tea together. At a second party, when the new mother was able to sit up, the visitors came again, bearing homely gifts, as it might be bread, butter, sugar or a little wine.

Far less decorous was the custom of riding the stang. This was a punishment for several crimes, such as wife or husband beating, or adultery, and was generally performed by proxy. Briggs had seen the ritual. 'The last time we witnessed an exhibition of this kind was for this crime.' (ie adultery.) The business could really only be carried out if the whole village was united in wishing it. The individual nominated to personate the culprit was, on a designated night, borne on a pole (stang), ladder or plank on men's shoulders from door to door. A large shouting retinue of men and boys accompanied the 'rider' who explained the cause of his appearance at each door in obscene doggerel, and concluded by begging money to spend. The last stop was at the culprit's door, which could be risky. Then the party adjourned with more shouting to the village inn to spend the beer money they had collected.

**Note**
Most of the material contained in this chapter, whilst not specific to Torver, is characteristic of the remoter parts of Westmorland and High Furness in the mid-18th century, and is taken from a series of annotated articles in the monthly *Lonsdale Magazine* of 1822 (printed and published by J. Briggs, Gazette Office, Kendal).

*Chapter Eleven*

# Torver Church

During the Middle Ages Torver was a part of the parish of Ulverston, but very little can be discovered of the early history of St Luke's church. There was a building in which the inhabitants were accustomed to worship on the site of the present church. Sometime during the reign of Henry II (1154-89), Gamel de Pennington granted to the newly established Priory of Conishead 'the Church of Ulverston with its chapels and appurtenancies'. According to the Rev. T. Ellwood (*Leaves from the Annals of a Mountain Parish*, 1888), the church at Torver was one of the chapels included in this gift. In view of the long distance from Ulverston and the difficulty of the way, over mountains and boggy ground, with streams liable all too often to floods, it was clearly a reasonable arrangement that there should be a place set aside for public worship in the village. Not until 1538, however, when Thomas Cranmer was Archbishop of Canterbury, was a licence given for the consecration of the chapel and graveyard.

This came at a time when other changes were affecting all the churches of England following Henry VIII's break with Rome. Torver was a remote corner of a remote parish, but ripples from the huge stones being cast into the ecclesiastical lake at that time must have disturbed the immemorial traditions associated with the celebration of mass and the administration of the sacraments. Yet there is no record of any local controversy. Perhaps most of the local people were so fully involved in the exacting business of making a living that they were prepared to accept without question whatever changes of church order were imposed. Perhaps many of them did not care overmuch, anyway: although their ancestors had accepted the externals of Christianity for many generations, their hearts would still be given to the older beliefs partly recorded still in place names and lingering traditions. To this day there are places in the parish more numinous than the church.

Be this as it may, a scrap of information from 1650 indicates how 'old fashioned' still were the ways of the parish. A puritan report of that year refers to the 'reader' as 'Sir' Roger Atkinson. This 'Sir', as a style of address for clergymen of the most ordinary sort, had long been obsolete over most of England. It survives in Shakespearian references (*As You Like It* and *Twelfth Night*) as almost the last recorded usage. With a name like Roger Atkinson, the probability is that this reader was of a local family; if he were, then problems of survival might have been made easier for him, because there was no endowment, and he had no maintenance except what the inhabitants raised themselves. Quite apart from financial problems, there must have been doctrinal ones in these turbulent years. Again, there is no direct contemporary reference, but it would seem obvious that the establishment of the Baptist chapel at Sunny Bank in 1678 was linked with the presence in the chapelry in 1717 of

63

Presbyterians and Anabaptists. Surely some of their more intransigent grandparents would have been raising knotty questions of heavenly obedience and civil disobedience in Commonwealth times. One feels that there would be occasions when Roger required all the resolution and awkwardness of which the Torver Atkinsons in other circumstances had shown themselves capable.

In September 1632, however, an Atkinson had been the plaintiff in an action which today would have been certain to attract wide publicity. Thomas Atkinson, husbandman, almost certainly from Moor, complained before Roger Kirkbye, Justice of the Peace, that Robert Place, clerk, of Torver, had 'beaten, strucken and dangerously hurt him', and in consequence, he was now 'afraid of further bodily hurt or harm'. Kirkbye issued a warrant to all the neighbouring constables to arrest Place so that he could be made to appear at the sessions 'to be holden at Lancaster after the feast of St. Michael the Archangel next ensuing the date hereof'. If Place refused to find good and sufficient sureties for his peaceable behaviour until then, he was to be conveyed to His Majesty's gaol at Lancaster. It has not been possible to trace any other document relating to this lively altercation, so we can only speculate that Place, himself of a choleric disposition, had been exasperated beyond endurance by his turbulent parishioners. The circumstance that in the next year another case involving Place came before the Quarter Sessions lends credence to the suggestion. He and his wife Agnes were brought to trial for disturbing the peace in brawling with a John Atkinson, who cannot be identified with certainty because there were so many men of that name in Torver in the 1630s. All three were indicted for the offence on 8 August 1633, and on 30 September both sides were, in effect, bound over for £20.

From 1688 the regular list of incumbents begins, with Edward Walker, who married Rachel Park, a local girl, 10 years later. The greater amount of documentary material relating to the 18th century makes it possible to reach out more effectively to the people of those times. The parish in 1700 had four 'quarters' – Hoathwaite, Stable Harvey,[1] Greenrigg and Torver Park. These quarters took turns in providing someone to fill the office of churchwarden, and their existence would make for administrative convenience in the collection of chapel dues. The burden of maintaining a minister would have been proportionately greater in those days than at present. The parishioners raised £5 1s. per annum to provide the curate's salary, or, to use their own term, 'priest wage', a phrase which does not suggest that they had an excessively mystical or exalted view of the office. In addition they would have to find another pound or two each year to meet the churchwarden's accounts, as well as financing occasional improvements or major repairs by special efforts. The earliest record of such an activity is for 1708, during the brief curacy of Andrew Naughley (1707-1709), when the chapel was 'paved with flagg stones at the cost of said town, with the consent of the sidesmen and churchwarden'. Edward Park of 'Roslathorns' filled that office, and his sidesmen, neatly representing the four quarters, were William Whinfield, Edward Jackson, James Wilson and Joseph Park. The operation seems to presuppose that hitherto the chapel had not been paved at all and that its interior would be like that of many of the parishioners' homes, beaten earth covered with dried brackens.

Through the churchwardens' accounts, presented annually, it is possible to build up a picture which illustrates the age in which they lived, and at the same time establishes a continuity with the present. The churchwarden had to keep an eye on all the practical details involved in the smooth running of the parish. Until 1835, when a parish clerk was first appointed, he had to undertake the bell-ringing and the dog-whipping. The farmers, who would feel indecently undressed without a long stick and a dog or two at heel, would leave these accoutrements outside at service time, so there was always a possibility that disputes would break out at inappropriate moments. For this occasional but exciting duty the churchwarden usually received one shilling a year; bell-ringing, being more onerously regular, was more amply remunerated. The emolument rose from 2s. 6d. per annum in the 1740s to 10s. 6d. in 1808. Another duty was to see that the surplice was washed regularly. No doubt the churchwarden's wife was often called in to deal with this one, pounding the garment over a stone in one of the becks, and then spreading it out over a hedge to dry.

Then the church premises and surroundings had to be maintained in good condition. Sometimes a window had to be glassed, or the churchyard wall repaired. Regularly, the church had to be mossed, eg. 1698, 'to getting of moss and mossing church, 5/6d.' Mossing was filling in all the chinks in the stonework of the walls so as to keep out the winter winds. The walls, although thick, would not be made of dressed stone, but of rounded and irregularly shaped cobbles with a clay and rubble infill. Another regular responsibility was to obtain rushes to spread over the flagstones on the floor. In 1744, for instance, 'rashing' the church cost 5s. 0d. Internal decoration required frequent consignments of lime, brought up by the bushel from Penny Bridge, at the mouth of the river Crake, eg. 1732, nine bushels, for 6s. 9d. Sometimes there was hair, or more often sand, to be mixed with the lime, just like Wall in *A Midsummer Night's Dream*. Leading (bringing by means of a horse-drawn cart) and getting stones and slate usually refers to necessary maintenance, although the year 1728, during John Hall's incumbency, provides an exception. William Wilson of Grassguards included in his accounts (in addition to 'slate, flaggs and stones'),

> 1/6d for flagg stones for seating the yows
> 1/0d for stones for walling yows about
> 4/4d for six days work about the yows.

*Torver churchyard and walled yews.*

The flags could well have come from the flag quarry just beyond High Barn, on the way to Tranearth, and the yews and their walls are still in the churchyard, although not, unfortunately, the seats.

The office of churchwarden circulated widely amongst the farmers in each quarter, indicating that most families in the parish were willing to be actively associated with the church. A sample round of the quarters runs:

|  |  |
|--|--|
| 1709 | Robert Fleming, Southerstead |
| 1710 | William Wilson, Undercragg |
| 1711 | John Atkinson, Houthwaite |
| 1712 | Thomas Parke, Oxenhouse. |

These men were all ordinary farmers; some must have lived very near the poverty line. Torver was not a wealthy parish, and it contained no gentlemen's residences. No one even approached affluence, although the extensive rebuildings of the 18th century all testify to a gradually rising standard of living, at any rate for the independent farmers.

Since there was no parsonage, the minister had to find accommodation where he could. His way of life and his standard of living must have been little different from that of his parishioners. John Stoup, who succeeded Naughley in 1709, is described as teaching the children in the chapel, as Edward Walker had done. Like Naughley, he inscribed an appropriate Latin paragraph in the parish register when he entered upon his ministry, adding a prayer which by its tone immediately makes us think more highly of him. In translation it reads, 'Humbly I pray to God that it will please Him to give me grace and blessing, by which I may be able to fulfil my duty to His glory and praise and majesty to the end of my life. Amen.' He was, it seems, 'a careful and diligent minister', who administered the sacrament of the Lord's supper twice yearly, and kept a wary eye on the Anabaptists and Presbyterians.

Stoup's successor when he moved to Coniston in 1716 was Thomas Poole. Torver was a lonely row to hoe, where a man needed all the grace and blessing he could get. Poole, whose curacy lasted for only two years, must have thought so when a serious complaint was made, through a sidesman, that the claims for chapel dues, for priest wages, were unfairly assessed – 'a very unequall way', they declared, 'of rating the said inhabitants, of which several have been thereby oppressed, especially those of the poorest sort, whose small estates have been charged equally with those of the greatest value.' Small estates, indeed, and the whole contribution only amounting to just over £5 a year. The curate was the man with the smallest estate, in the midst of these spikily independent and close-fisted Vikings. It wasn't as if there were any worthwhile fees to supplement the wage. Poole's pen burned into the register as he noted them precisely:

For wedding, tenpence if asked in Church
For Christning one penny, and Churching twopence
For burials, sixpence.

He could have buried the whole pack of them for a year's wages!

In fact, the anxiety of the parishioners was primarily a longstanding concern over their financial obligations towards the parish church in Ulverston. From time out of mind, Torver, along with the other dependent chapelries, had contributed to the maintenance of the roof and wall of the mother church. The earliest extant documentary evidence is a receipt for 8s. dated 1680, towards the cost of such work. Not an onerous burden, it would seem; but the receipt for 1713 was for 16s., and in 1714, £4, in respect of which the receipt was pointedly worded: 'The whole sum of four pounds of lawful British money, being their full proportion of a sess laid for the repair of roof and walls of the Parish Church of Ulverston, according as they are obliged by former custom.' Four pounds was a fair sum of money at a time when a sheep was valued at 4 or 5 shillings. Then for 1719 there is another receipt for £8. The people of Torver must have known that this further big bill was imminent at the end of 1718, and this circumstance would lend urgency to the representations of no fewer than 11 local farmers 'as well upon their own behalf as on the behalf of several other inhabitants' to the bishop's commissary.

Their successors continued to be slow payers throughout the century, and lost no opportunity to reiterate that the roof and walls were the only part of the parish church to which they were liable to contribute. There was rather a problem, therefore, in 1775 when representatives were summoned to a general vestry meeting in Ulverston to consider whether a new vestry should be erected. So great and inconclusive was the debate that in the end they sought counsel's opinion. John Wilson of Howe, Troutbeck, advised that the representatives were entitled to attend the meeting because the construction of a new vestry would create additional walls. They were on this ground entitled to vote against a proposal which would increase the area of roof and wall. There was no question of Torver being bound to contribute to the cost of building a new vestry, because ancient custom referred only to repairs. After all, Torver had its own chapel to maintain. This was altogether a highly satisfactory verdict. The Torver share of the 1778 repair bill of £23 2s. 8d. was identical with the Coniston share, at £1 9s. 6¼d., which suggests a diplomatic as well as a meticulous division of the cost. Yet they never stopped niggling about the business. As late as 1811 G. S. Holroyd of Gray's Inn was reinforcing the obligation as a moral if not certainly a legal one: 'I think that the inhabitants of Torver are liable to pay towards the repair of the churchyard wall and gates. Payment of the rates can I think be enforced only by proceedings in the Spiritual Court.'

They weren't such bad people though, as John Hall, who followed Poole in 1718, was to find over the next 16 years. The most remarkable event of his curacy, considering its financial implications, was the purchase and installation of a new bell, cast in Dublin, which weighed 252lb. The cost 'for stocking thereof besides the old bell' in 1730 was £16 4s. 10d. The Torver folk would pay up if they were really interested. The cash was raised by a 'sess', or rate levied equally on the parish, and Ellwood recorded that the bell was still in use in 1908. This notable acquisition suggests that Hall possessed both diplomatic talent and strength of character; but by direct reference, there is little in the contemporary sources about either his character or interests. He regularly helped in dealing with wills and inventories, which he wrote in a neat hand, always using a special little flourish to mark the 'H' of his surname.

When Hall left in 1734, young Robert Walker held the curacy for a couple of years. Despite the great reputation for industrious sanctity which he later acquired at Seathwaite in Dunnerdale, he seems to have made little impression on Torver during these prentice years. His great-grandson, the Rev. Robert Bamford, in a memoir, observes that Torver, being pleasantly situated on the banks of Coniston Water, was capable of affording more of the comforts of life than Buttermere, where his position over the past three years had evidently been little more than that of schoolmaster and lay helper. This may well have been so, but Robert had left his heart in Buttermere, or rather, the vale of Lorton, even though he had applied for the vacant curacy of Torver. He had left it with Anne Tyson of Brackenthwaite, and languished simultaneously for Anne and for Seathwaite where he had been born and brought up, even as he was lodging, comfortably enough, with one Higham, a butcher, who does not appear in any other document relating to early 18th-century Torver. Bamford sums up the situation with circumlocutory delicacy:

> Having prevailed upon a decent young woman, for whom he had contracted a tender regard, to relinquish her duty in Buttermere, he had almost determined to enter into the marriage state immediately. But delaying a little longer in the expectation that Seathwaite might want a pastor, his wishes to obtain the situation were gratified. For though Torver was on all accounts to be preferred, yet Mr. Walker had such a partiality for Seathwaite that he voluntarily gave up all pecuniary considerations, married, and took his wife there.

The wedding took place on 5 January 1735/6 at Dean church, near Workington, and later that year the parishioners of Torver welcomed another young man as their minister, John Hartwell. The tone of the replies that Isaac Atkinson from Hoathwaite made as churchwarden to the bishop's visitation questions in 1737 seems to indicate the general pleasure in having a minister whose mind was on his job, even though he was clearly very inexperienced.

> We have a young man at present to supply our Chapel, who designs to offer himself for deacon's orders at the first opportunity ... He reads the prayers of the Church, provides that the sacrament be administered as usual ... being not ordained, wears not the surplice ... visits the sick, instructs our youth in the Church catechism, bids holy days.

John stayed until 1740, when, with the arrival of Robert Bell, there began an era which may be unique in the parish annals of England. Between 1740 and 1911 only three incumbents served Torver.

Bell's ministry lasted for 67 years. For a great deal of this time he lived at Scar Head, reputedly in the cottage at the sharp bend in the road just across from the old swill shop. In his later years he became blind, and the parish register entries are made in another hand. When Bell's name is entered, the Latin word *caecus*, meaning 'blind', is placed after it. During this incumbency (1777) John Fleming (probably of Coniston) left money for the founding of an English grammar school. Soon afterwards a building was erected near to the church. Bell had been involved in the local agitation which had been going on for some years before Fleming's death to provide more satisfactory schooling in the parish. He also figures from time to time as witness to a will, or assisting the highway surveyors when letters had to be written, but, like John Hall, he remains a rather shadowy figure. The churchyard sundial, set up in 1744 at a cost of less than £1, including board and drink for the evidently abstemious workmen, but removed already when Ellwood arrived in 1861, seems a sadly appropriate memorial.

Bell's successor, Matthew Carter (1807-64) emerges more fully, perhaps because, with the 19th century, documents become less scarce. The successive churchwardens, of course, continued their ancient routines, as in the beginning. From the 1808 accounts, for example,

For washing surplice and cleaning cups, 3s. 0d.
For sweeping Church and dressing churchyard, 2s. 0d.
For repairing Church windows, 2s. 4d.

Carter himself had a university degree and until 1819 acted as master of the new parish school. He must have had a taste for rural life – for 20 years he farmed about 40 acres at Brackenbarrow. Shades of Wonderful Walker here, but Carter was of a much more quiet and retiring disposition. He lived in several places after giving up his farming, at Rosley Thorns, for example, where he is recorded in Parson and White's 'Directory' for 1829. He was evidently very fond of walking, and would hike across to Kendal – all of 20 miles – after evening service. This seems to be both an odd time and an unexpected destination. No doubt the explanation is that he was visiting other members of his family, who lived in Kendal and with whom he spent Monday as his day off, before hiking back to Torver. Sometimes he walked to Elleray, too, in what is now Windermere, but was then a tiny hamlet looking over the lake. As an old man he told Ellwood that John Wilson, the critic and litterateur who wrote under the pen-name Christopher North, had been accustomed to spend a good deal of time there during the early years of his own incumbency at Torver, and that he used to visit him frequently. Part of the attraction must have been the presence of persons like Wordsworth and de Quincey. 'For a considerable period', wrote Ellwood (*Forty Five Years in a Mountain Parish*, 1908), 'Mr. Carter used to associate with them, and he has told me much of what they said and did at Elleray.' Maddeningly, that is the end of Ellwood's note.

However, it was during Carter's incumbency that the old church disappeared. In 1849 the lime-washed, flagged, bemossed structure was replaced at a cost of £200 by an up-to-date building in the Early English style, large enough to accommodate 200 persons, ie. everyone in the parish – 199 parishioners were enumerated in the 1841 census. A. C. Gibson in 1849 commented that a very neat and appropriate chapel had just been erected. It is to be hoped that this work really was a crown to Matthew Carter's ministry, for an account of 1860 (Wright, Cumming and Martineau) gives a generally depressing picture of the chapelry. The living, in the patronage of Messrs. Petty and Postlethwaite of Kendal (maybe the minister went to report to them after evening service), was worth only £59 a year. The incumbent lived 'in a most miserable house, on the side of a mountain, about a mile and a quarter west by south of the chapel', Souterstead, in fact. Finally, the school was attended by only 10 children.

Fortunately, perhaps, when the Rev. Thomas Ellwood first visited Torver in 1861, with a view to assisting, and eventually taking over from the now ailing Carter, the sun was shining and the birds were singing. He soon made the acquaintance of the parish clerk, who doubled as the village joiner and lived opposite the kirkhouse. Before the day was done, Ellwood had determined to give up his teaching post at St Bees school and come to Torver. The brightest period in the history of both church and parish was about to begin under the guidance of this able and energetic scholar. Ellwood has written the only extant systematic description of Torver. He was a prominent member of the Cumberland and Westmorland Archaeological and Antiquarian Society, and was widely known as an authority on Icelandic studies. He was moreover an efficient and dedicated minister, whose primary concern was always the church he served.

In 1861 there was no shortage of work for him to do. 'The clerk told me', he recollected later, 'that Dissent was making rapid inroads in the parish, and that there had been no singing in the Church, or none to speak of, since the Church was restored in 1849.' Descendants of those pesky Anabaptists, or maybe some were sneaking off to the Primitive Methodist chapel in Coniston, where we may be sure the singing was lusty enough. However, the immediate problem was a material one. A 'miserable house' was no credit to the Church or its Creator. After having officially become incumbent in 1864, on Matthew Carter's death, with the encouragement of his archdeacon, Ellwood began his campaign for a parsonage. It was an uphill struggle against entrenched attitudes. He later recollected:

> I spent a whole day in going about and bringing my 'powerful plea' before the parishioners, and after calling on most of the ratepayers, and doing my best to influence them to help me by laying my case before them, I found at night when I came home that what I had got or had promised amounted altogether to 18s. The day's round did me a great deal of good, however. The parishioners were not at all backward in giving their advice, or at times in expressing their disapproval, and in replying to them and urging the matter upon their notice, I was warmed up to go on with the work.

He worked to such purpose that in 1866 Torver was declared a Rectory, and not long afterwards the fine south-facing house situated just off the Coniston road, below Brackenbarrow, was built. The land was given by Mr. W. Barratt of Holly How, Coniston, owner of the then flourishing copper mines. The next job was to rehouse the school more satisfactorily. Finally, attention had to be directed to the church itself, because the new buildings of Carter's time had proved a dreadful disappointment. By the late 1870s it was apparent that the walls were giving way, and an architect's report pronounced them dangerous. Ellwood describes in his little book, *Forty Five Years in a Mountain Parish*, how he set about the huge task of organizing the rebuilding, completed in 1884.

The cost of the new church was about £1,300. There was little inflation in those days, so this figure means that it was almost seven times as expensive as the Early English structure of mid-century. The Barratts of Coniston and the Robinsons of Brown Howe responded handsomely and cheerfully to this third appeal to their public-spirited benevolence. It was a great help also that Messrs. Mandall, the local quarry owners, donated the stone; that the parishioners carted this stone gratuitously; and that the Furness Railway Company conveyed other building materials free of charge. On the whole, however, the local response seems to have been less than overwhelming. Analysis of the accounts shows that £110 of the £1,120 raised was donated by persons who can be positively identified as ordinary Torver parishioners. This £110 includes £12 5s. from three concerts, £5 3s. from a tea in the schoolroom, and rather more than £38 from sundry collections made in church and school. It was not as if the 'locals' had already given sacrificially to the rectory building fund. There had been two donations of £5 each in a total of nearly £940. Somewhere or other, the shade of Thomas Poole must have been chuckling sardonically. Yet Torver was now a more prosperous place than it had ever been. The coming of the railway partly explains this – thanks to the better communications, there was more industrial activity: quarries on the moor, manufactories at Sunny Bank and Greenrigg, and tourists were beginning to arrive by the carriageload. In a word, Torver was sharing in the greater national prosperity of the later 19th century.

But basically the drive and the organising ability behind the rebuilding of the church had been Ellwood's. He was determined that his parish should no longer be the backwater it had been regarded as in earlier years.

Ellwood's own description of the opening service in the new church, conducted by the bishop, Harvey Goodwin, gives a marvellous vignette of his own admirable worthiness, along with a certain lack of a sense of humour, or lively imagination.

> The Church was crowded, many being unable to obtain admission. Upwards of twenty of the neighbouring clergy were present, including the archdeacon, the rural dean and others. The bishop took as his text Matt. IV/63, 'And Jesus went about all Galilee, teaching in their synagogues'. From these words he preached a most impressive and eloquent sermon; dwelling especially on the advantages derived by scattered mountain parishes by having a church in their midst. The tea which was afterwards partaken of in the schoolroom was most numerously attended, all the parishioners seeming to turn out to it in a body.

During the later part of his incumbency, as his health began to fail, Ellwood was assisted by his son, the Rev. R. D. Ellwood, who acted as curate, and eventually took over full responsibility. Since that time the most notable rectors have been J. B. Panes, J. Redman and R. S. Heaton, of whom the last named sustained the longest ministry, over a period extending on each side of the Second World War. Imperceptibly, through these years, as the old ways of life dissolved, the church ceased to be the focal point of the community. Torver people came to look more frequently outside the parish for their work, and more people from outside came to live within the parish, not all of them 'weekenders' or the retired. Easier travel did more than anything else to break up the old patterns, so that Torver became part of a wider, but more loosely knit community. One symptom of this was that Torver was placed under the pastoral care of the vicar of Coniston in the early 1960s, so that nowadays, alas, there is no separate and resident rector of Torver.

### Text of notice to attend a meeting about assessments in relation to the cost of repairs to Ulverston Parish Church, 1718

*18th December 1718*: Peregrine Gaskell, Commissary of the Archdeaconry of Richmond to William Wilson, Chapelwarden, and inhabitants of Torver to meet and make a rate for repairs to Ulverston Parish Church.

Whereas complaint hath been made unto us by William Wilson, Roger Whinfield, Matthew Carter, Caleb Wilson, John Park, James Wilson, Miles Fleming, Edward Park, Joseph Park, Robert Wilson and William Brown, inhabitants within the chapelry of Torver; as well upon their own behalf as on the behalf of several other inhabitants within the said chapelry, that irregular and undue methods have of late been taken in laying and charging assessments within the said chapelry for the repair of the Parish Church of Ulverston and the chapel of Torver aforesaid, under the pretence of rating according to the method of raising the Priest-wages within the said chapelry, which pretended custom by experience hath been found a very unequal way of rating the said inhabitants, of which several have been thereby oppressed, especially those of the poorest sort, whose small estates have been charged equally with those of the greatest value, not only contrary to law and equity which require that the rates should be charged in proportion to the several values of the estates, but also to the great delay of the necessary reparations of the said Church and Chapel:

In order therefore to redress the grievances aforesaid: these are to ... enjoin order and require you to give public notice in the said chapel on Sunday next after date hereof, that the inhabitants within the said chapelry are required to meet in the said chapel on Friday 26th day of December instant at eleven o'clock at the toll of the bell, and then and there to proceed to make a rate for the repairs of the Parish Church of Ulverston and of the deficiencies of the said chapel of Torver, ... in proportion to the value of the estate of each inhabitant of the said chapelry ...

The notice ends with instructions for the collection of the assessment.

### Churchwarden Accounts, 21 June 1743

Then did John Jackson being Churchwarden for his Estate at Brackenbarrow for the year 1742 give in his accounts to the Sidesmen as followeth:

|  | £ | s. | d. |
|---|---|---|---|
| For a book | | 5 | 6 |
| A journey to Ulverstone | | 0 | 4 |
| Rushing Church | | 1 | 0 |
| for a Prayer Book and Proclamation | | 1 | 6 |
| for Washing Surplice twice | | 0 | 8 |
| Spent in Ale upon Workmen | | 0 | 6 |
| for a Bell rope | | 0 | 3 |
| for Bread and Wine | | 7 | 4 |
| to Richard Lowther | | 1 | 0 |
| Nicholas Prit | | 2 | 10 |
| for Glassing windows | | 2 | 4 |
| 2 Journeys to Cartmel Fell | | 1 | 4 |
| A Boss for Church | | 0 | 6 |
| for Boatage of Freestone | | 1 | 0 |
| half a Day Work | | 0 | 6 |
| Six Hoops of Lime | | 0 | 8 |
| A Journey to Cartmel | | 0 | 8 |
| for Ringing Bell | | 2 | 6 |
| Commissary[2] Fees | | 8 | 10 |
| For Mending Churchyard Wall | | 0 | 4 |
| Smith Work | | 9 | 11 |
| for a New Door &. | | 14 | 2 |
| For Writing Return of Articles & a Sess Bill | | 1 | 6 |
| In all | 3 | 5 | 2 |
| Remains in Leonard Parke[3] Hand undisbusted[4] | 1 | 8 | 3 |

### Churchwarden Accounts for the Division of Torver for the Year 1808

|  | £ | s. | d. |
|---|---|---|---|
| Bread and Wine | | 18 | 0 |
| Bell Ringing | | 10 | 6 |
| Wishing [sic] Surplice & cleaning Cups | | 3 | 0 |
| Repairing Church windows | | 2 | 4 |
| a jurney to Ulverstone | | 2 | 0 |
| Spent | | 2 | 0 |
| Righting Regester | | 1 | 0 |
| Sweeping Church & dressing Churchyard | | 2 | 0 |
| Commissary fees | | 11 | 4 |
| | 2 | 12 | 2 |

(The churchwarden for the year 1808 was John Massacks of Church House.)

## The definitive statement following the great row about chapel dues in 1718
April 11, 1718

Chapel dues belonging yearly to the Curate of Torver, granted out of the old Church rolls, and stated according to each individual's proportion:

| Hoathwaite Quarter | s. | d. |
|---|---|---|
| John Atkinson sen. | 2 | 2½ |
| John Atkinson jun. | 2 | 2½ |
| Myles Fleming Grassguards | 3 | 0 |
| Richard Harrison | 1 | 3 |
| John Jackson Brackenbarrow | 2 | 9½ |
| Edward Park eiusdem[5] | 1 | 4¼ |
| William Wilson eiusdem | 1 | 1 |
| William Wilson High Steel | 2 | 7 |
| Elizabeth Gardner | 1 | 6½ |
| James Wilson | 3 | 2 |
| R. Parke Roslethorns | 1 | 7½ |
| Mr. James Biggland Emhall | 1 | 9½ |
| | | |
| £1: 4 | | 1¼ |

| Torver Parke Quarter | s. | d. |
|---|---|---|
| Roger Fleming | 3 | 6½ |
| William Wilson Undercragge | 1 | 6½ |
| Agnes Wilson Moor | 3 | 0 |
| William Atkinson sen. | 5 | 0 |
| William Atkinson jun. | - | - |
| Matthew Carter | 2 | 7½ |
| William Whinfield | 6 | 0½ |
| Idem[6] Scarhead | 2 | 0 |
| Myles Fleming | 1 | 1½ |
| Thos: Birkett | 1 | 7½ |
| Jno. Fleming | 1 | 4 |
| Edw. Jackson | 1 | 7½ |
| William Fleming Parkyate | | 2 |
| Low Close | | 2 |

| Stableharvey Quarter | s. | d. |
|---|---|---|
| John Parke | 2 | 2½ |
| Richard Parke Jun. | 1 | 1 |
| Tho: Parke for a parcel of an estate bought of Joseph Penny | | 10½ |
| Richard Parke for do. | | 1½ |
| Rowland Parke Roslethorns do. | | 6 |
| Luke Browne for do. | | 8 |
| Matthew Coward for do. | | 4 |
| Matthew Coward | 1 | 1 |
| Luke Browne | 9 | 11½ |
| Will: Atkinson Thrangcragge | 1 | 0 |
| James Kirkby Brownhow | 1 | 4 |
| Rich: Lowther | 1 | 6 |
| Tho: Parke Stableharvey | 1 | 6 |
| Rich: Parke | 2 | 1 |
| Tho: Parke   eiusdem | 2 | 4 |
|                    Meadow | | 5½ |
|                    do. | | 9 |
| | | |
| Rich: Parke for parcel of said estate | 1 | 4 |
| Mr. James Biggland for Mill | 1 | 2 |
| Roger Whinfield | 4 | 3 |
| James Park Park Ground | 3 | 5 |
| Agnes Wilson Moor | - | - |

| Greenrigge Quarter | s. | d. |
|---|---|---|
| William Jackson Heslehow | 2 | 4½ |
| William Atkinson Garthnook | 1 | 3 |
| William Wilson Graves Gd. | 1 | 11½ |
| Jane Brown eiusdem | 1 | 11 |
| Anthony Atkinson | | 10 |
| Tho: Atkinson | 1 | 3½ |
| Tho: Walker | 2 | 4 |
| Will: Atkinson Greenrigg | 1 | 4½ |
| Robt. Fleming | 1 | 9 |
| Edward Atkinson | 3 | 5 |
| Blawith H . . . | | 0½ |
| Tho: Brocklebanke | 1 | 0 |
| Heslehow | | 1 |

All these amounts were determined 'according to the joint agreement and consent of the Churchwarden, Sidesmen and major part of the inhabitants'.

*Chapter Twelve*

# Torver Charities

An undated memorandum in Torver parish register states:

> That old Michael Atkinson of the Bankend in Torver did give unto the fower quarters of the said Torver one tyn bottle for to remayne at the Church, and to (lend) to everie one at tyme of (need) or when one is sicke to seke a lytle aqua vitae or wyne and to bring it again unto the Church, without any rest or denial of the same and of yt I make supervysors Leonard Parke wife, Rychard Parke wife, George Atkinson wife of Greenrigg and Wm. Atkinson wife of Souterstead to se it kept w(ell).

This picturesque benefaction probably dates from the mid-17th century. George, son of John Atkinson of Greenrigg, was baptised in 1615, and Leonard, son of Thomas Parke of Church House, in 1617/18; but it has not been possible to discover for how long the tin bottle remained, suitably replenished from time to time, in the church. But the homely gesture does Michael Atkinson credit, and places him chronologically at the head of the short list of charitable donors in Torver. The parish never had close associations with any really wealthy person, and the population was so small in numbers that statistically it was unlikely that any of its sons should leave home and make a fortune.

Exactly what had been John Middleton's connexion with Torver is not clear from the wording of his will in 1685. He had lived in the hamlet of Thwaites, near Millom, at Greystone House, but he left a portion of his estate to four Torver executives – Roger Whinfield, Leonard Parke, John Atkinson of Hoathwaite and Richard Crowdson – 'to bestow the yearly interest of what sum they receive [it turned out to be £37] by virtue of their executorship ... to charitable and pious purposes within the parish.'

John Woodale (or Woodvill) of Whitehaven, whose will was proved in 1730, is more clearly local in his connexions. He had been a mariner, but in all his journeyings had never lost touch with Torver friends and relations. He appointed his uncle, William Wilson of Greaves Ground, to be his executor, and made a number of personal, as well as charitable, bequests.

> I leave to my executor or his heirs to dispose of for the use of Torver's poor the sum of £15 for good and charitable uses as he shall see good for to do, as to paying for the learning of poor children and buying them books. I leave to John Parkhouse and John Atkinson the sum of £15 for the use of Sunny Bank Meeting to dispose of as they shall see good to do, and after them their heirs ...

The personal bequests include £3 to his aunt, Ann Wilson, £5 to Jane Park and her daughter Lydia, three guineas to his cousin Agnes Wilson of Greaves Ground, and £5 to Mary Park of Sunny Bank, another cousin. It seems reasonable to deduce that Woodale had no family of his own, and that his spiritual sympathies inclined towards those Anabaptists[1] whose presence in the chapelry had been noted in the ecclesiastical visitation of 1717, although his charitable bequest is recorded on an old wall plaque preserved in the church.

74

Elizabeth Fleming was as local as it was possible to be. A widow when she died in 1742, she had lived at Grassguards just behind Brackenbarrow. After a rather complicated proviso which hinged on her nephew's daughter, Mary Jackson by name, dying without issue, she left £2 to the sidesmen of Torver, the interest to be divided amongst the poor. It was a very small legacy, but Elizabeth had known poverty at first hand, and lived amongst people never very far above the line which divides poverty from want. Personal beneficiaries under her will included William and Alice Wilson (20s. each) who lived at Grassguards. William, along with James Pritt, also of Grassguards, who made his mark, and Isaac Atkinson, witnessed the will.

In this mid-18th century flowering of charitable intentions, no one was more magisterial or so detailed in his specifications as Samuel Towers, nor so devoted in his concern for the welfare of the established church. Perhaps John Woodale's £15 had been doing wonders for the morale of the Sunny Bank dissenters. The relevant detail follows, verbatim.

### A Copy of that part of the Will of Samuel Towers deceased which relates to the Money given to Torver Curacy and which was by the said Will to be copied on parchment and kept in the Church Chest there Viz:

Item I give to the Township of Torver in the County of Lancaster forty pounds to be secured on free land or to be let to interest, and three responsible persons to be bound for the same, the interest of which shall be paid out yearly for ever as follows, Viz: To the Curate of Torver seven shillings and sixpence yearly for preaching a sermon every Easter Monday or Tuesday for ever; and to the Clerk of the said Church one shilling, and to the Sexton sixpence yearly for ever: also to the Churchwarden and Overseer of the poor each of them one shilling yearly for ever for their care in the due execution hereof, and it is my will that all the remaining part of the Interest of the above Money be laid out in buying Common Prayer Books of Tate & Brady's new version Psalms, till every house have two or three at least that are of this Church of England and to be allways supplied with same sort as they shall need for ever; and the said Curate, Churchwarden and Overseer of the poor than shall buy Bibles or other Books of Devotion with the rest of the interest Money and divide them equally to all alike: and it is my will that the Clerk shall set out to be sung part of one Psalm line by line forenoon and afternoon when Psalms are sung for the better Edification of old people and mean scholars; and that the said New Version Psalms be sung instead of the old for ever, and further it is my will that the Curate or Parson of Torver do teach and oblige all the children of Torver as soon as capable to get by heart the 103rd Psalm to the nineteenth verse of the New Version for ever; and it is my will that fifty shillings be advanced by my Executor over and above the forty pounds abovementioned to fit out the said township with New Version Prayer Books at present.

Robt. Bell, Curate
Edward Parke, Churchwarden & Sidesman
George Ashburner, Sidesman
Ishmael Wennington, Sidesman

There was no delay in carrying out these instructions. The parson and the officers received their first payments in 1758, and 38 copies of Tate's Psalms were bought in the same year from Mr. Ashburner for £2 10s. The only definite link that can be traced between Towers and Torver is that in 1731 'Samuel Towers of Bootle' owed £1 7s. to David Fleming, saddletree maker, of Undercrag.

A board in the old church recorded further charitable donations to the poor of Torver. The board was pulled down in 1848, but the Rev. T. Ellwood subsequently made a copy of its content, as follows:

|                        | £  |
|------------------------|----|
| Given from Rydal       | 5  |
| By Wm. Fleming         | 30 |
| John Atkinson          | 5  |
| Dorothy Jackson        | 4  |
| James Pritt            | 3  |
| Anthony Atkinson       | 5  |
|                        | —— |
|                        | 52 |
|                        | —— |

Robt. Bell - Curate
Wm. Fleming - Chapelwarden
1754

|                       | £  |
|-----------------------|----|
| Given by Rowland Atkinson | 5  |
| Thomas Atkinson       | 5  |
| Mr. Ambrose           | 17 |
| Henry Fleming         | 5  |
| John Whinfield        | 5  |
| John Atkinson         | 5  |
| William Fleming       | 10 |
| Elizabeth Fleming     | 2  |
| Anthony Atkinson      | 5  |
|                       | —— |
|                       | 59 |
|                       | —— |

Joel Park - Churchwarden
1738

Some of these donations are really very handsome if they are compared to the resources of the givers, whose families, if not their individual identities, can all be found in the parish registers of the time. Mr. Ambrose is the exception. The Ambroses lived at Lowick Hall, eight miles or so down the Crake valley towards Ulverston, and, as further evidence of their benevolent propensities, the Rev. John had left bequests for the poor of Blawith and Lowick about 1685. The entry, 'Given from Rydal' will refer to the Fleming estate, centred on Coniston Hall for generations, until the then recent move to Rydal.

Sometimes a charitable donation was more specific than simply 'for the poor'. The scanty emoluments of the curate occasionally benefited from charitable donations, not only in money, as in 1717 when W. Fleming gave £30, and J. Fleming, J. Atkinson and the 'Gentlemen of Ridall' £5 each to augment his annual stipend of £7 1s. In 1754 Robert Bell signed in the presence of the sidesmen (Edward Parke, Daniel Fleming and Richard Lowther) that he had received, and would eventually hand on to his successor, the following books:

Stackhouse's 'History of the Holy Bible', 2 vol., folio
Nurse's 'Homilies', 1 vol., quarto
The Book of Cannons [sic]
The 39 Articles
Stanhope on the Epistles and Gospels, 4 vol.
Nelson's Festivals and Fasts, 1 vol.
Altham's Sermons, 2 vol.
Gastrell's 'Christian Institutes', 1 vol.

The books are included in an undated inventory from later in the 18th century, in which the four at the end of the list are marked as the legacy of Dr. William Stratford, 'for the use of the curate of the chapel of Torver'.[2] One hopes that the quality of the Rev. Bell's homilies gained from his study of these works, and that some stimulus and comfort percolated through to the church floor, so to speak. Dr. Stratford appears in 1759 also, when the church of Torver was augmented by the purchase of lands for £400, of which £100 had been given by 'the executors of William Stratford, Ll.D.' 'His interest in Torver', Ellwood observed in a passage of his book where experience of his own seems to surface in sympathy with his predecessor, 'seems to have sprung from a disinterested desire to improve the lot of whoever had to sustain the curacy of this, the most distant, and, as it must also have seemed, the least rewarding corner of his "parish" '.

Only one other large charitable donation was ever made to the poor of the parish, that of Ann Kilner, whose will was proved at Ulverston in 1851. The tone of this will is significantly different from that of Middleton or Woodale, reflecting the Victorian attitude towards 'the poor' as a sort of social institution provided for the more fortunate classes to exercise their benevolence on. Ann Kilner bequeathed to the churchwarden and overseers of the township of Torver 'wherein my mother was born ... £100, the interest to be divided equally amongst six poor women residing in the said township who shall not be then in receipt of parochial relief, such poor women to be selected by the said churchwarden and overseers along with the incumbent.' The surviving records show these instructions being carried out, with the names of the 'poor women' and the amount each received set down carefully year by year. The same names crop up every year for a period, with an occasional omission as the changes are rung, then disappear for good. Every so often there is a personal note that lights up a situation or a character. In 1889, for example, the vestry meeting showed its opinion of Mary Bayliff by minuting that her money (11s. 7½d.) should be paid by Mr. Ellwood 'at the rate of one shilling per week, or such larger amount as he may think proper'. The pencilled notes underneath show that Mr. Ellwood did not think it at all proper, because he doled out the cash in shilling instalments over a period of three months.

There is no evidence at all to suggest that the charity monies were ever mismanaged or misappropriated, but in Torver, they all knew each other, and tended to go on doing things in the way that things had always been done. William Wilson looked after the Woodale accounts in the early years of the 19th century, as a member of his family always had done, after his own fashion, but not in a way to suit His Majesty's Charity Commissioners, who reported of the Woodale charity in 1820: 'As no accounts are kept of the distribution, and the money is given away by one individual only, we have recommended that a more public distribution should take place.' Of Middleton's charity, it was observed: 'Neither does it appear that the inhabitants of the division are aware of this charity.' However, they were prepared to allow Wilson to continue directing operations, for there was no suggestion that the monies had ever found their way into his own pocket. It was just that he had been doing things his way, and indeed the Commissioners recognised that he had been giving away about 12s. 6d. a year in money, meat and books to the poor.

Then Daniel Birkett acted as secretary for many years through the mid-19th century, and he knew, everyone knew, who held the different monies, and how much interest was due annually. But again these homely arrangements did not satisfy the strict requirements of the Charity Commissioners, who in 1860 must have got round to having another look at their Torver file. W. G. Hayter, the Commissioners' accountant, sent to Daniel Birkett on 4 August a summary of the charity monies, as follows:

| Charity monies held by | | £ |
|---|---|---|
| | John Birkett | 160 |
| | John Park | 40 |
| | Joseph Tyson | 215 |
| | On mortgage | 50 |
| | | ——— |
| | | 465 |

BUT, the principal sums are,

| | | |
|---|---|---|
| Kilner | 90 | |
| Towers | 40 | |
| Woodale's | 15 | |
| Middleton's | 50 | |
| Poors money | 60 | |
| School | 215 | |
| Lent to J. Parker | 10 | (donor unknown) |
| | 480 | |

Hayter followed with an inquiry as to how the £15 difference was secured: 'I am at the same time to point out that this most unsatisfactory disposition of the charitable trust monies cannot be sanctioned, and to request that all these sums may with all convenient speed be called in and be properly invested in the Government securities.'

This brisk and business-like tone was very much in the spirit of the age, but it was altogether too much for Daniel Birkett who replied as follows on 18 August:

Sir,
  I beg to be excused as I will be 74 years of age the 17th Dec., and having been a cripple for upwards of 50 years, and am under the obligation to engage a clerk to answer your letters, I hope you will look over me for the future and direct to the Overseer, and you will oblige,
Yours truly, D.B.

One can imagine the consultations that must have taken place, Daniel saying 'Who does this man think he is? We've been running it this way for the last 50 years, I'm not going to have anything further to do with it, not at my time of life', and then the arm-twisting necessary to persuade someone else to take over. They must have succeeded, because the next surviving communication from Mr. Hayter dated 15 May 1868, is addressed to Mr. William Parker of Hazel Hall. William had evidently continued to show the traditional disregard for any requirements of officialdom, because the letter begins:

Sir,
  The accounts of the above charities for the past year being now some time overdue, I am to call attention thereto, and to request that the same may be made out and transmitted without delay ...

There had nevertheless been some move towards conciliating the Commissioners since 1860, because now the investments were allocated as follows:

Income from mortgage of houses and land, £220
Furness Railway Company, £200
Trustees of the late Thos. Wilson, £50
In Wakefield's bank £1 19s. 2d.

It is interesting to note that these sums still do not add up to the £480 which had been Mr. Hayter's point of concern in his original letter of 1860. The Rev. T. Ellwood, naturally, saw to it that every detail connected with the charities was as clear and correct as possible. Take the Middleton bequest, for example, with which in his day the Bank End Wilsons were associated. The Wilsons' connexion with this charity was, in a sense, accidental, because the principal was secured on mortgage of copyhold land of which they were the owners. In his little book of 1888 Ellwood observes primly that 'Mrs. Mary Wilson pays the interest to an annual Vestry meeting held for the purpose of distributing charities and distributed then in accordance with what the Vestry consider the most deserving cases.'

Indeed the charity accounts continue to show the wishes of all the benefactors being observed, regardless of whether anyone in London was satisfied with the way that the forms were being filled in. The monies were distributed until 1964, even the annual sixpence to the sexton, following a meeting of the responsible officers. The most unusual aspect of the charity distributions is that associated with Samuel Towers. Although there is no means of finding out when the Torver children no longer had to learn psalm 103 by heart, it is possible to trace what happened to the book distribution from the time when Tate and Brady had become old- instead of new-fashioned. By the mid-19th century the income from the Towers bequest was being used to buy for general distribution throughout the parish various other suitable publications. In 1852 it was Prayer Books, in 1860 a *Companion to the Bible*, and in 1865 *A New Manual of Devotion*, 40 copies purchased. A household could gradually accumulate a small library over the years.

Consider the Barratts, who lived at Hoathwaite throughout the second half of the century. The records show not only the titles bought (eg. 1883, *Hymnal Companion to the Book of Common Prayer*, new and enlarged edition, 8¼d. each; 1887, *Holy Communion* by the Bishop of Bradford, 8d.; 1890, Bibles, 'Nonpareil', published by the S.P.C.K., one shilling) but also the names of each individual recipient. From 1852 to 1897 Sarah and Alfred Barratt acquired nine Prayer Books, nine *Hymnal Companions*, one Prayer Book (long primer), two *New Manuals of Devotion*, one *Family Prayers* and one *Holy Communion*. One resident, whose family has lived in Torver for several generations, replied, when questioned about these books, 'Oh yes, we've got a whole boxful of them'. A *Hymnal Companion to the Book of Common Prayer* now in the possession of Mr. R. Prickett of Hollace, has a bookplate inside the front cover inscribed as follows: 'Capt. S. Towers Charity. Presented to the House of Thomas Kendall at Ellice How Cottage. Distributed by Rev. T. Ellwood. March 29th 1892.'

As a small coda to this continuing stream of books, Bibles were also distributed from the Ulverston-based Sawrey bequest at irregular intervals between 1858 and 1893. In the latter part of the century Ellwood appears to have used this charity to enrich his confirmations – nine in 1890, and 17 for the first confirmation service to be held in Torver church in 1893.

No record exists of books being distributed in the 20th century. Indeed, by the 1960s social conditions had changed to a degree that made it possible to rationalise the parish charities in general. But for a period of three centuries they had contributed to the sum of material well-being in the parish, and had helped to bring the village folk closer together in the administration of shared and constructive purposes.

## Chapter Thirteen

# Torver School

The beginnings of a system of formal instruction for the children of Torver are not recorded. Many of the later 17th-century inhabitants could read and write, and probably their schooling had taken place in the church. In a sample of 28 wills and inventories from the next generation (between 1701 and 1743) there are the names of 64 individuals, of which 11 are distinguished by 'his/her mark'. This must be partly a tribute to the work of the Rev. Edward Walker who ran a school in the church, rather in the style of his illustrious namesake who later moved across to Dunnerdale and in Seathwaite church contrived simultaneously to spin his wool and instruct the young. At any rate, in 1693 a licence had been granted by the ecclesiastical authorities for the curate to be master of a school in Torver. Bishop Gastrell's report of 1717, known as the *Notitia Cestrensis*, noted that although there was no endowed school in the township, the curate taught in the chapel. The wills of both John Woodale and Samuel Towers later in the 18th century testify to the continuance of this arrangement, and to the keen interest taken in the village school at least by some folk who, looking back, saw that they owed the first steps in what had turned out to be a successful career to the instruction that they had received there. But as time went on, and the general level of prosperity in the whole area rose, the feeling began to develop that something more was needed, that the existing provision was fair neither to the children, who were denied the amenities of a proper school, nor to the curate, who might have no talent for teaching.

In 1777 the Rev. Robert Bell and 24 of the parishioners tried to give substance to these general feelings. On 21 December they sent a carefully worded petition to Elizabeth, Duchess of Buccleugh, lady of the manor of Muchland (in which Torver was situated), offering to forgo claims to the wood of Torver Common, and requesting that a portion of the proceeds of the wood be used towards endowing a school. They claimed:

> It hath long been lamented, and with deep concern felt, by your petitioners, and the inhabitants of the said Manor, the want of a school, or seminary of education, adjoining to the said Chapel, for the rearing and bringing up of young children to read and write: there being neither public nor private school within the said Manor, nor any nearer than at several miles distance; and that a benevolent gift, or liberal donation, from the Lady of the Manor, would be a great furtherance and encouragement to your petitioners, and the inhabitants within the said Manor, as also the adjacent neighbourhood, liberally to contribute therewith; proportionably to their industrious endeavours, to enable them to endow and support a school for the purposes aforesaid.

It is not clear whether this petition had been sparked off by John Fleming's will of 1777, or whether John Fleming was influenced by all the talk of a school that was in the air about that time. However, he acted, whilst Buccleugh Estates, so far as can be ascertained, simply noted. Perhaps the petitioners had chosen their time badly, and at Christmas there had been many other calls on the ducal liberality, or maybe their excessively deferential tone and apparently uncontrollable urge to say everything twice over succeeded only in boring Lady Elizabeth to tears.

Fleming's action was to bequeath £200 to Thomas Dixon, William Fleming and Edward Atkinson as trustees, to be placed out at interest which should then 'be applied and paid towards establishing and supporting an English Grammar School at Torver, for the schoolmaster there for the time being'. The precise wording is significant. 'English', not Latin grammar was to be the subject in which the young were to be instructed, so there would be minimal consequent risk that a little learning might give the children of the peasantry ideas above their proper station. Fleming further directed that if the schoolmaster should be negligent, the trustees should withhold the interest, and that the trustees should appoint as many poor scholars to be taught free as they should agree the greatest objects of charity. It was not until 1790 that a school was built on a piece of waste ground by the roadside adjoining the church, a paltry building on a mean site. The earliest reference to a schoolmaster by name is in 1804, when the trustees paid £8 to John Coward, schoolmaster. Also in 1804 they appointed to be taught free for a year 'a child of the late Edward Atkinson [one of the original trustees], and one of John Fleming's'. Each year thereafter, two, three or four children, by no means always boys, are named in the Fleming Schoolmaster Charity accounts: for example, after half a century, in 1854, 'Robert Walton, John Fleming, Isabella Crewdson and Betty Pattinson, to be taught free for reading'. A further bequest which had been made in 1820 by John Birkett of Crook helped to make this kind of provision rather more generous. Forty pounds was left for Daniel Birkett and the Rev. Matthew Carter to place out to interest, this interest to be applied 'in paying the quarterage schooling for poor children born of parents belonging to the township of Torver, and educated at Torver school, kept by a master of the Established Church, within the township'. At this time Carter himself had been acting as schoolmaster for a number of years, so the old tradition had been maintained, as it was later to be, through the Rev. T. Ellwood's keen interest in the school.

However, Ellwood's first acquaintance with the school, in the early 1860s, came at a rather unfortunate stage in its history. The comment in Wright, Cumming and Martineau's account of 1860 is to the effect that 'there is a school near the chapel, possessing a small endowment, and attended by about ten children'. A note pencilled on the back of the 1860 correspondence with the Charity Commissioners, respecting the schoolmaster's living, strikes an even gloomier, albeit somewhat confused, note.

> Two years ago there was £40 payed up which was in the hands of Danl. Birkett, that money loses 6s. a year and the schoolmaster having the expenses to bear in changing the money, which amounts to 19/10d. Now how his [sic] the schoolmaster to live? He has only 18 scholars, and out of them six are free and all coming to the school that are capable in the parish. There is only three counters, and their quarterage is 7s. 6d. per quarter each, five writers at 5s. each and three readers at 3s. 6d. per quarter. Now if the school money was laid out on land security it would be the means of keeping the schoolmaster in the parish; if not it will be an inconvenience to the parish, as there will be nothing for a schoolmaster to live upon.

Inconvenient for the schoolmaster too, one feels! But if the hand which wrote the memorandum was not particularly lucid, at least it was concerned. And, fortunately, there was at that time a strong personality at the beginning of a long association with Torver who would share that concern, and from his position of influence and authority change the situation of the school out of all recognition.

His first encounter with rural schooling was not propitious: the Rev. T. Ellwood, in his *Forty five years in a Mountain Parish*, describes the experience vividly. The year was 1861.

> I went into the parish school, close at hand. The master was out, and that was taking place which generally does take place in schools and some other public places when every man, or every boy, is left to do that which is right in his own eyes; there was, in short, a scene of considerable uproar and considerable noise. All this subsided, however, into an intense silence when I got myself fairly inside. I asked when the master would come back, but as they didn't seem to know, I first took a few observations of the school, and then proceeded to ask the scholars for any information I could get. It was certainly the smallest school I had ever seen, and also, as far as I remembered from its building and equipment, the worst I had ever seen. The floor was in great measure paved with rough cobblestones. Small as it was, a boarding made up of very rough and unsightly wood still further contracted it.
>
> The most remarkable things about it, however, were the seating and the grate – the seats were for support let into the wall, and in this way with the weight of the scholars, acted as levers, and it was, as I found out afterwards, not an unusual circumstance for the end that was in the wall to give way, and for the form and the scholars all to go down together. In the way of interest, the grate was the masterpiece. As I learned afterwards, the heating had originally been carried out by a hearthfire – ie., a fire on the hearth without any grate at all. It would have been much better to have kept the hearthfire arrangement. Someone, however, who was getting a new grate, for this grate had apparently been presented to the school in its last stages, had given this grate to the school; and, to make matters worse, it had been set up by an amateur who, apparently, had had his first, and as I should hope, this, his last, grate-setting job here, for he had set it in such a way that the smoke came into the school instead of going up the chimney. The master therefore, in cold weather had the alternative of having a fire, by which he was half suffocated, or no fire, when he was equally sure to be half starved [chilled to the marrow, an old Northern usage]. Under these conditions, he was 'out' sometimes ... I left the building and the scholars, eighteen or twenty in number, with a strong impression that whatever might be requested elsewhere, something, by curate or incumbent, was evidently required to be done here.

With characteristic energy, Ellwood set about doing something right away, but he soon came up against the deeply ingrained local indifference to schooling and suspicion of schoolmasters. 'There seemed', he wrote many years later, 'so much local fault finding, and so much, I thought, unnecessary criticism, that I at last gave it up in despair ... It was not until 1870 [ie. following Forster's important Education Act of 1870], that we received an impetus and had to make efforts that compelled us to go through with the work. Before carrying it out I had tried to obtain a school two or three times over, and two or three times all that I could do seemed to have been done in vain.'

There were two alternatives for the parishioners, assuming that they did not wish the school to be closed. Either they provided a new school, of the required standard (in the official inspection of school buildings made after Forster's Act, the existing school was pronounced to be incapable of repair, and altogether unsuited for the purpose of a school), or they submitted to the machinery of establishing a School Board. This second alternative would have meant a regular school rate, and would also have removed the school from the influence and authority of the church. Ellwood disliked this aspect of the Board solution as much as most of his parishioners detested the thought of a school rate, so he began a vigorous and successful lobbying which soon produced satisfactory results. Mr. W. Barratt of Holly How, Coniston, subscribed 20 guineas. Then, 'J. Robinson Esq., of Brown How, Torver, most generously made the offer that he would double whatever I could raise by voluntary contributions from the parishioners, or others in the neighbourhood.' This had the effect of doubling the sum of £62 13s. 6d. which Ellwood had drummed up from other well-wishers. Work began forthwith on a piece of ground which Mrs. Massicks gave to enlarge the site on which the old school stood. Mrs. Massicks was the widow of Isaac Massicks who for many years in the mid-19th century kept the Church House, and whose home-brewed ale was so rapturously acclaimed by A. C. Gibson in his *Ramblings and Ravings round Coniston* in 1849. The visible evidence of work in progress stimulated further gifts, so that by 1873 the new school was completed at a cost, including the site, of about £350. The premises were conveyed to the rector and churchwarden for the time being in trust to be used for the purposes of a Sunday School and 'a public elementary school for the instruction of children and adults, or children only, of the labouring, manufacturing, and other poorer classes in the parish of Torver'. The trustees were responsible for the expenses incurred in the day-to-day running of the school, and for the administration of charity monies directly associated with the school.

Ellwood composed a hymn for the official opening on 28 May 1873, which was sung again on 28 November 1914 when an extension to the premises was opened by the Bishop of Carlisle:

> God of Heaven in mercy hear us,
> Bless our efforts in Thy name ...

Looking back from the distance of over 30 years later, Ellwood could feel a justifiable satisfaction, as if indeed a special blessing had rested upon this work. The school was running more smoothly than at any time in the past, and the charitable bequests were being administered in a manner guaranteed to meet the most exacting requests of any Charity Commission accountant. He wrote:

In 1907 the income from the Fleming bequest was £5 11s., and from the Birkett endowment, £1 2s. 4d., which was paid by the trustees to the schoolmaster on the first Tuesday after Easter. In respect of this payment, the trustees nominate annually three poor children (generally on the ground of their being members of large families) to be educated free of charge during the year, the school not being entirely free, but a weekly fee of 1d. being charged in respect of half the children for the whole year. The school is conducted as a Church of England public elementary school, and has an average attendance of thirty five.

The penny a week seems odd, as late as 1907, when acts of parliament had long ago decreed that elementary education should be both compulsory and free; but Establishment circles in these remote rural areas have always been in favour of self-help on the part of the labouring classes, and Torver school never succeeded in freeing itself from the taint of charity. The trustees in 1907 were Ellwood himself and W. H. Heelis, the Ambleside solicitor who married Beatrix Potter. Ellwood never taught in the school, but was a man of considerable learning. He made it his business to help any scholar of the school in further studies, along with the private pupils he took from a wide area, even to university entrance level, provided that the youngster had both the interest and the necessary academic ability.

During the 20th century, the history of the school has been one of decline which no one could have foreseen on that triumphant winter day in 1914 when they were celebrating the opening of the enlarged school premises. Decline accompanied falling population, and the move towards ever-larger administrative units, which, in the name of cost-efficiency, finds good reasons to dispense with small local institutions that are expensive to maintain simply because they are in remote places. Torver school was closed by the Lancashire County Council in 1927 and the pupils transferred to Coniston, travelling in those days by rail. The gaunt rectangular school building continued to house adult education classes until the 1970s. Now it serves only as the village hall on the rare occasions when some public event takes place in Torver. The biggest and liveliest of these events, fortunately, still involves the children – the annual Children's Sports, when the glass and wood partition across the interior is folded back and the place is filled again with the kind of cheerful clamour that greeted Ellwood in 1861.

* * *

Ellwood compiled a list of schoolmasters of Torver school, without, however, noting the dates of any of their appointments. This list, with comments by the author, is transcribed below.

1819 Rev. M. Carter relinquished schoolmasterly responsibilities. Thomas Kendal who succeeded him, lived at Lowick, five miles down the Crake valley in the direction of Ulverston, and walked daily into Torver.
Edward Park and George Park – both of that branch of the Park family then based on Brocklebank Ground.
Rev. J. Steble
Abel Fleming – he who was out when Ellwood first called at the school in 1861.
George Parker
John Knight
Christopher Airey – almost certainly of Greenrigg, where in the 1870s Ellwood used a room for regular public worship.
James Bowerbank
W. White
Joseph Lund
George Watson
Joseph Lund [see opposite]
George Watson
Augustus Rhees
Simon Dixon Brown
F. G. Binns
H. Bullock – he held the post in 1907, and in the local Directory for 1903 is recorded as living at 'The Larches', Souterstead; at that time he had an assistant, Hannah Barrow.
Miss Copsie [see opposite]

It is interesting to speculate why there should have been such a large number of schoolmasters in the second half of the 19th century. From 1861 to 1907 their average tenure of office was no more than four years apiece. Were they mainly young men for whom this appointment was the first stage in an unfolding professional career? Did some of them become resentful of the limitations inescapable in teaching on such a small stage with such scanty and unpromising material? Was Ellwood so big a fish in so tiny a pond that his all-pervasive influence suffocated anyone with the least degree of independence, or, more bluntly, was he impossible for the average person to get on with?

*Joseph Lund* is a man who appears elsewhere in local records, and one who probably didn't care a button whether he got on with the rector or not. He was already a schoolmaster when he undertook the secretaryship of the newly formed Sawrey Co-operative Society in 1875. Nine years later, when the Society had expanded the scale of its operations, he added to his responsibilities by taking over as manager of the Society's recently established Coniston branch, combining this with his secretaryship until 1886. Mr. Lund was a man of many parts, who would try his hand at anything, within reason. He lacked the singleness of purpose which had ensured the promotion of his predecessor at Coniston to the general managership of the Sawrey Society. As well as running the store, he took in clock repairs privately, and undertook commissions as a photographer. There wasn't enough time for him to attend to every detail, and in 1887 it was discovered that the books didn't balance. There was no suggestion of dishonesty. It was just that Mr. Lund was unable to account for over £70. In the next year he resigned his managership, perhaps feeling that confining himself to the mastership of Torver school would give him more time for his hobbies.

*Miss Copsie* was well remembered by some of the older Torver people in 1980. After Mr. Bullock left, the school became a single-teacher school, and Miss Copsie was that single teacher until the closure in 1927 when the numbers had fallen to about fifteen. She was an able and conscientious person, if perhaps inclined to be rather pedantic. However, she succeeded in passing on to her pupils her own deep sense of personal responsibility as well as the good manners that she valued so highly. In those days it was a great thing for any of the country children to win a scholarship to the Ulverston Grammar School, and Miss Copsie's pupils brought off this feat on several occasions. In order to give promising pupils the best chance, she used to arrange extra lessons for them at her home of an evening. This is perfectly understandable at 50 years distance, but at the time did not go down well with some of the local parents whose offspring were not selected for the special tuition. She also gave coaching for specialist examinations, most notably from her own point of view, George Postlethwaite, much younger than herself, whom she married in 1927. Maybe this marriage sparked off the decision to close the school, for at that time married women did not stay in their posts.

## Chapter Fourteen

# *Industrial Activities*

The principal industry associated with Torver has always been slate quarrying, although in 1980 no quarries were being worked within the parish. When Joseph Budworth stopped at Coniston in the course of his fortnight's ramble to the Lakes – the year was 1792 – a local guide named Creighton offered to take him to the summit of Old Man. 'We did not stop to hesitate; but we had the precaution to take some brandy, and at one o'clock began the arduous task ... There are several slate quarries upon this mountain. I looked in at one near the summit; there is a gallery to it, and it is arched like an immense gothic roof.' Originally, slate was extracted *ad hoc* in small quantities from any suitable place near to the point where the stone was going to be used. Rough building stone was easier to find than slate for roofs or flags for floors and corners of buildings, because these two uses required special stone: for slates it had to cleave easily in the right thinness, and for flags the stone had to lack that grain which was so necessary in making roofing slates. The old houses still have their flag floors, and the flags would come from one of the small flag quarries, such as that above High Barn on the road up to Tranearth. The earliest documentary reference to flags is in 1708 when a note in the parish register reads: 'This chapel of Torver was paved with flag stones at the cost of the said town, with the consent of the sidesmen and churchwarden'.

Systematic quarrying on a relatively large scale dates only from the 19th century, when the general demand for slate increased nationally, and a transport system was developed by means of which such heavy products as slate were no longer limited to a very local market. Even when the railway was available to producers, the dressed slate still had to be brought down from the quarries, high on the moors, by horse and cart to the station yard. Mr. Harold Grisedale, who worked at carting slate from Ash Gill as a youth, remembered in 1980 the difficulty of the journey and how muddy the roadway was as it approached the valley floor through the woodland behind Little Undercrag. The highest quarry of all was Goldscope, operated by the Kendal family, just below the summit of Brown Pike, reached by a track leading off towards Blind Tarn near the top of the Walna Scar pass. Mr. Gordon Kendal (1983) recalled the equable temperature and constant supply of water dripping from the roof inside the working level. He and his father did all the work themselves, even making most of their equipment, and engaged a specialist workman when one was required – perhaps for carting finished slates down to the railway wharf. Ash Gill, famous to geologists, is situated in the broad hollow of the High Common, on the north side of Ash Gill beck. At both these sites the workings were extensive, and there remain the ruins of various stone huts and shelters as well as big spoil heaps and quantities of 'quarry bottoms', the little pieces mainly chipped from the corners of slates as they were being shaped. The biggest of the Torver quarries, however, was at Eddy Scale, where some of the workings are across the border in Coniston parish. To a greater extent than at the other two quarries, the ground here is fairly level, so the slate was extracted not from a face cut into the hillside, but from a vertical-sided hole in the ground, of ever increasing size as the years went by. The big hole on Bannishead Moor is spectacularly melancholy, containing now a darkly ruffled lake, into which a wind-blown waterfall continually patters. Mr. E. Dickinson of Undercrag recalled in 1980 how on one occasion his father was returning home after dusk, following a visit to friends over in Dunnerdale at Turner Hall. He knew the way well enough, and was not alarmed even when his horse stopped and refused to budge. However, he dismounted, to discover that he was standing on the very edge of this gloomy chasm.

*Slate gate post with bars in place.*

The different quarries each produced a distinctive type of stone. C. M. Jopling, in his *Sketch of Furness and Cartmel* (published in 1843 by Soulby of Ulverston), observed that in some of the Coniston quarries the slate was of a dark lead colour, while in others it was of a light green. 'At Torver the colour and beds are various, and alternately flaggy and cleavable. The Walna Scar slates are of a light colour, and show many curious shifts in the stripes.' The Eddy Scale quarry was responsible for the poor reputation that Torver slate came to have. It is dark in colour to begin with, and, used in any quantity, makes a building look oppressively heavy and forbidding. Worse than this is the fact that after a time it begins to break up. Local walls made from Bannishead slate in the heyday of the quarry are now no more than untidy heaps of broken fragments. Ash Gill slate, by contrast, is of a high quality and an attractive light green colour, rather similar to that produced from the later Broughton Moor levels. Pieces of it give a pleasantly metallic clink from the boot soles as one moves over the quarry site. A good local illustration of the contrasting stones is at Green Cottages, which the Railway Company faced on the front, which could be seen from the train, with superior green, whilst at the back is the darker slate.

In their working arrangements these quarries were primitive in the extreme, with no provision for the comfort of the quarrymen, and very little for their safety. Some of the ruinous stone structures at each place would shelter the rivers and the dressers.[1] Other buildings even provided spartan living accommodation for the workmen who came to Torver by rail and lived at their workplace through the week. From Bannishead at least it was not far down to the road by which the slate was carted past Scar Head into the village to reach the amenities of the Kirk House or the *Miners Arms*. Local workmen had to set off on foot from about 6.00 a.m. onwards to their work, some of them calling en route at the little stone huts where they kept a few hens, to arrive at the quarry face for 7.30. The evening journey downhill was a rapid clatter taking less than half the time needed for the morning plod. Jopling had a proper respect for the quarrymen, which filters through his rather patronising tone. 'Although once notoriously intemperate, many have found the advantages of sobriety, and the demoralizing "quarry drinks" are nearly abolished. Some parts of their work require great steadiness of head and perfect coolness and command. Their work naturally leads them to think, and they, and the miners generally, are an intelligent race.'

These old quarries were worked by small groups of men acting fairly independently, under the general direction of one of their number. Today, they are desolate, even grim places. When they were in full production, these quarries were much less lonely. Jopling noted how the rattling of rubble and stone down the sides of the hills, and the incessant clatter of the slate-rivers' hammers, gave the appearance of great activity. He was very impressed by the drama attendant upon blasting operations. 'All the arrangements of boring and charging having been completed, the signal for the workmen to retire is given by the vociferation of the word "fi-er", which is immediately answered by all tools being laid down, and retreat being made to a place of security.'

Until very recent times quarrying was a labour-intensive industry. The large pieces thrown down by a blast were themselves bored and blasted until reduced to manageable proportions, after which further hard work with the aid of sledge-hammers and wedges was required to produce pieces which could be carried away to the riving shed. Here the river split the stone into thin sheets, a highly-skilled operation, needing considerable dexterity and a good eye. Finally the dresser converted these thin wafers into slates by shaping them with a special heavy knife. The slates were then stacked in rows according to their size and thickness. The classification, recorded by Jopling, was into Londons, Countrys, Toms, Peggys and Jerrytoms, Londons being the best. From the quarry the slate was carried in horse-drawn carts, either to a lakeside quay, or, later, to the railway stations at Coniston or Torver.

Mr. Claude Cann, son of one of those Cornishmen whose mining skills had contributed so much to the prosperity of 19th-century Furness, was the founder of the biggest industrial enterprise ever to be associated with Torver. By the mid-1920s Mr. Cann was already an experienced and knowledgeable quarryman, and he was anxious to establish his own business. At that time the principal requirements for establishing a new quarry were a strong right arm and a nose for finding out where the slate was. Although others had prospected fruitlessly on Broughton Moor, adjacent to the Torver parish boundary, Mr. Cann was convinced that further investigation would be worthwhile. Along with two other quarrymen, Messrs. O'Mara and Mellon, he surveyed the desolate moor in minute detail. They eventually spent their entire savings in the enterprise, with no more success than any of their predecessors. As a final gesture, almost of despair, Mr. Cann suggested tunnelling in the opposite direction, where they had previously reckoned that there would be no workable slate. So, at the last moment, they struck the huge deposit of high-quality green slate which has become known as the Broughton Moor quarry.

From this small beginning, with a handful of men, the quarry grew rapidly in size, so that 10 years later, in 1939, over 100 men worked there, and it was not uncommon for 450 tons of finished roofing slates to be produced in a month. Even when Bannishead quarry had been in full production, Torver had never known such economic prosperity. Mr. Cann's son, Arthur, worked tirelessly to convince architects that this richly-coloured, slightly-cambered slate was equal to anything else of its kind, visually attractive, and durable enough to resist atmospheric pollution.

Demand for slate did not fall off with the Second World War; indeed, there were some unusual orders, such as the one for 2,000 tons of roofing slate for the army camp at Catterick, the colours to be as mixed as possible so as to act as camouflage. At this time German prisoners of war were drafted in to supplement the labour force, because the extraction of slate required a vast expenditure of muscle power. Only three to four per cent of the rock extracted is usable, so enormous quantities of waste have to be shifted to the spoil heaps. In addition to this tedious and heavy work, the finished slates, rived and dressed in stone-built shelters on the quarry site, had to be carted down to the railway loading wharf. The carters worked in pairs, each with three horses, and they would load 15 cwt. of slate on to a cart, with an additional half ton on a sledge behind. In the quarry itself they had bogies running on metal lines through the tunnels to the quarry face, and crab winches to help with lifting big blocks of stone. One of the greatest skills was to place the boreholes in which explosive was to be detonated so as to bring down the least quantity of rubbish in proportion to workable material, and at the same time to minimise the shattering that would destroy this material.

None of this was so very different from the scenes described by Jopling a century earlier, but after the Second World War the quarry had to adapt to meet the needs of a changing market, and to cope with higher labour costs, which put a premium on mechanisation. In 1947 Mr. Cann revolutionised extraction techniques by perfecting what may be described as the 'big blast' method. They excavated a 40-foot tunnel, with two 30-foot arms at the end, making a T-shape. Then they sawed with a wire rope at the base of each arm, so that the rock below would not shatter, packed tons of explosive into the tunnel, sealed off the entrance, lit the fuse, and retired to a place of safety. The ensuing explosion brought down 100,000 tons of rock and debris, and when the dust had settled, revealed that Mr. Cann's intuition had been right again. The new method had brought down a greater proportion of usable rock for the craftsmen at a considerably reduced outlay in labour.

By this time, however, the craftsmen were not only, or even primarily, concerned with making roofing slates. Architects all over the world were coming to see the possibilities of using slate as a cladding material. So Torver slate was used extensively in the post-war rebuilding of Coventry – at the Cathedral, in facing new buildings in the shopping centre, and for the ceremonial foundation stone of the new city. One of Broughton Moor's earliest coups outside Britain was to face the Imperial Bank of Commerce in Montreal, a building 600 feet high, for which 1,200 tons of finished slate were required. This type of order has in more recent times come to be the quarry's staple product. As operations have become increasingly mechanised, the size of the labour force has diminished, in line with the declining population of the village, and today's visitor will hear the sound of huge earth-moving machines rather than the clatter described by Jopling. Nevertheless the quarry, now part of the great Burlington Quarry group, remains as a reminder of the long industrial traditions of the village.

Slate was not the only mineral to be extracted from this moorland. The narrow band of Coniston limestone passes across the High Common, from a point below High Pike Haw on the south side, then above Ash Gill, and into Coniston below the Cove. In certain places the limestone outcrops and is easily recognised from its characteristic weathering, if not by its colour. Limestone was quarried in suitable places along this belt, mainly for farmers to use on their fields, according to local tradition. The pits rather than quarries consist of small smooth grassy hollows, made to seem larger than they really are by the upcast around their rims. Some of the biggest are to be found on High Pike Haw, where there is also a well-preserved kiln. The entrance to the kiln is high enough for four persons to shelter inside from a sudden snow squall and, from the grassy platform above, lumps of limestone could be fed through the aperture in the top. Whether this kiln was for lime burning, or for drying large pieces of timber for the mines or quarries, its existence at this spot presupposes that there must have been a fair amount of wood nearby for use as fuel or raw material.

The Ordnance Survey map marks another limekiln in the field above Tranearth, known as Fleming Tranearth. Investigation suggests that this may not have been a limekiln at all. It is very like several other similar structures in the parish – there are two, indeed, by the side of the road leading up from Little Arrow to Bannishead, and another in the narrow valley between High Pike Haw and the deer dyke. Each has a low entrance, facing south of east, and the body of the structure is shaped rather like a pudding basin. The type site for this kind of furnace could be the beautifully preserved one in Broughton Mills, immediately by the upper side of the road to Stephenson Ground from the bridge over the Lickle. They are potash pits, for burning bracken, coppice branches and brashings.[2] The otherwise pernicious bracken was harvested ('sheared') in the late summer. In the early 1970s one or two old people could remember ashes being taken to a little factory in Ulverston, and exchanged for soaps.

Many of the old tracks leading to the high quarries and the limestone diggings can just be deciphered and followed, particularly in winter when the vegetation is dead, and the low angle of the sunlight illuminates otherwise invisible lines across the landscape. Some of the tracks lead to former peat mosses, which continued to be actively exploited within living memory, on both the Low and High Commons. Every home had its peat house for fuel storage, and the annual rituals of cutting and stacking, then carting down on narrow horse-drawn sledges in the early summer, were as much a part of Torver life as they still are in the remoter Hebrides. Other tracks again lead into the woods, from which also regular harvests of fruits and nuts as well as winter fuel used to be gathered. But no tracks lead directly to any of the Torver bloomeries, a circumstance which lends credibility to the suggestion that there was something occasional and temporary, even perhaps shady, about their operation.

Along the lake shore bloomeries existed at Harrison Coppice (where there is also what has been described as a smelting hearth, but which looks suspiciously like another potash pit), at Moor Gill foot, and further south again, tucked away near Old Lee Coppice, above the shore behind Sunny Bank. Two further bloomeries may be found on the Low Common, the more remote in the upper part of the valley from which Mere beck emerges. The other site is on Throng Moss, overlooking Torver reservoir which was created in the 19th century to provide storage and a good head of water for the bobbin mill at Sunny Bank. The Throng Moss site is the most fully documented, as it was carefully examined and fully discussed by A. Fell in his *Early Iron Industry of Furness*. These bloomery sites are all similar in their characteristics. There is a heap of slag and cinders, up to 60 feet across, and eight to ten feet high, largely grassed over, but with considerable quantities of refuse (known as scoriae) littering the surrounding area, particularly where the bloomery had been by the lake shore. The biggest pieces have long since been removed for use as doorstops, or as curiosities to be put on the mantelpiece, but much remains scattered among the stones along the water's edge.

For a long time the bloomeries were known as 'Roman', but Fell's opinion is that they date from the period after Elizabeth I made commercial iron-making illegal on account of the terrific inroads that the industry was making into the forests. Iron smelting had taken place in Furness during the Middle Ages. The monks had maintained three 'smithies' in High Furness, which had passed on the dissolution to Messrs. Sawrey and Sandys, but none of these smithies can have been in Torver. However, the secluded and wooded nature of the area made it an ideal place for individuals to take advantage of a provision in Elizabeth's decree for tenants to set up small bloomeries for their own benefit, using only forest loppings and underwood as fuel. We must remember that four centuries ago the Low Common at Torver would not be the bare wilderness we see today. There would be plenty of 'dead' wood about, and no doubt the bloomery operators hastened the demise of suitable trees, as opportunity offered, thereby contributing to the creation of the present desolation. The interested passer-by will soon notice that the bloomery refuse is of two kinds, one heavy and very dark, almost black, the other much lighter both in weight and colour, due to the action of gases and water. Excavation of the Throng Moss bloomery revealed the entire hearth, 6ft. 6ins. in diameter. It was flat and open, showing no sign of heat, but to one side was a hollow, 1ft. 6ins. in diameter. This was the reducing hearth, and had a bottom of burnt clay. The procedure was to fill the reducing hearth with charcoal, and feed ore into it a bit at a time to roast, for all the world like cooking roast potatoes on bonfire night. The scoriae ran away, and the still impure iron was removed as a 'bloom' with the aid of tongs. The Throng Moss hearth did not even show evidence of any bellows to encourage the heat in the reducing hearth.

According to Fell, commercial iron making with the aid of water-powered bloomery forges was re-established by the third decade of the 17th century so the lifespan of these small and primitive bloomeries may well have been fairly short and, as the 17th century continued, they gradually ceased to operate. The 'refuse' from the slag heaps was still so rich in metallic iron that the cinders were later turned over to extract the best for re-use as flux in the newer smelting furnaces. It may well be, therefore, that the remains still to be seen are merely the final refuse heaped together after this recycling operation. The only evidence to suggest that the small bloomeries may antedate Elizabethan times comes from R. G. Collingwood, who, assisting his father in excavations before the First World War, found what appeared to be late medieval pottery in them. A cynic might observe that during the 19th century even, there would be plenty of people using what would have looked like late medieval pottery in Torver.

Part of the attraction for the bloomery operators was the quantity of thick woodland in and around Torver. This woodland played an indispensable role in iron making through the production of charcoal from coppice wood. Acres of this woodland, mainly hazel, remain, although now sadly neglected. The proper cycle of management was one of about 15 years, when the poles were cut systematically from the stools, and stacked by the level circular pitsteads where the charcoal burners conducted their operations. These pitsteads are about 15 feet in diameter, excavated slightly out of the slope above, and built up to a corresponding extent below. Nearby is sure to be water, and usually 'sammel holes', where the burners dug out clay soil to plaster over the smouldering pyres. These pitsteads abound in all the Torver woodlands, from Harrison Coppice near the lake shore to the broken ground above High Park where the land is no longer given over to coppice woodland. The charcoal, made up into bags, was carried by pack animals to such destinations as the bloomsmithies, and later to such voracious consumers as the iron furnace at Duddon Bridge, where the charcoal store is as big as a church. In the whole of the period through which the industry flourished, it was easier to bring the iron ore to the source of the charcoal, and then carry away the blooms of iron.

Here and there in the woods are the remains of the little huts which used to house the charcoal burners during their temporary sojourn in a particular coppice. These huts, familiar to any reader of Arthur Ransome's books, were circular in plan, consisting of a low, roughly built stone plinth, which incorporated a hearth, and from which sprang a high conical thatched roof supported on a single centre pole. It was convenient to distinguish areas of woodland by their owner's name, and Harrison is not the only resident to have been immortalised by the Ordnance Survey in this way; Kilner, Dixon, Johnny and George Wife were all coppice holders within Torver parish.

Some of the huts provided shelter for bark peelers. The woodland was of oak where it was not hazel. Oaks were managed either as standards, for timber, or as coppice. The bark peeler was concerned with oak as a coppice crop, and at the proper time, when the sap was rising, would remove the bark and bundle it for use by one of the local tanners. The uses to which the wood itself was put were legion. In addition to the purposes already noticed, there was the obvious one of providing fuel, although no one had the right to go into someone else's wood and help himself to a handy tree. As long ago as the Middle Ages, the Furness monks had clearly defined and limited the privileges of tenants in such matters as loppings and toppings, greenhew and brushwood. Then a multitude of useful domestic articles were made from wood in the days when iron and glass were expensive and plastics non-existent. Most of the 18th-century inventories include an entry under the heading 'wooden vessels'. The two products which came to predominate, however, were swill baskets and bobbins.

Greenrigg became a centre for basket making in the later 19th century. There was another swill shop below Scar Head, latterly kept by Mr. Jock Wilson, which was only partially ruinous in 1970 when the long iron trough in which the wood was soaked and boiled to make it pliable was still in situ in one of the compartments of the workshop. Basically, a swill consisted of a rim of hazelwood which anchored the interwoven oak laths that formed the body of the basket. They were very handy and light in weight, lending themselves to a great many uses – the annual accounts of the Torver Surveyors of the Highways from the 18th century record the occasional purchase of a swill, and no farm was fully equipped without them. The swillmakers therefore were less vulnerable than the bobbin makers, whose product required greater capital investment and served a more specialised market. The greatest prosperity of Charnley's bobbin mill at Sunny Bank coincided with the apogee of the Lancashire cotton industry. At the time of the 1851 census, William Kendal, woodturner, was the proprietor of a flourishing concern. There were six bobbin turners, and six apprentice bobbin turners, a sawyer and two servants. Interestingly, none of the apprentices was local. Two came from Egton-cum-Newland (Greenodd), and the others from Kendal, Kirksanton, Kirkby and Backbarrow respectively. When cotton began to decline, so did bobbin manufacture. By the 1930s most of the business at Sunny Bank consisted in meeting the local demand for such items as pick and hammer shafts, and for besoms,[3] and in making ships' fenders. Some of the machinery had been taken out before 1939, and since the war, the general use of plastic bobbins in the few remaining mills, along with the use of a cordon of old tyres along the sides of many ships, have prevented any hope of a resurrection. These words might serve as the epitaph on all Torver industries. In 1980 all that remained was a handful of home-based craft-type business ventures.

*Chapter Fifteen*

# Communications

In the 1980s Torver is not a place that the motorist would notice particularly, and certainly not as a route centre. From the north the road comes in from Coniston by a wide left-hand sweep over Brigg House bridge before dividing just south of *Church House Inn*. Here is a T-junction. The left fork goes over Hollace bridge, to take a sharp right turn beyond what used to be the post office-cum-village shop, then continues past the site of the pinfold up the hill to Greystones. Then the road takes a series of sharp bends before descending Sunny Bank hill quite steeply to cross Torver beck at Sunny Bank bridge. The straight and wide section of road bypassing Oxen House beyond the bridge is in Blawith. Back at the Church House the alternative road continues along the line of the old railway in the direction of Broughton in Furness until it rejoins the line of the original Broughton road south of the driveway to Brocklebank Ground. From this point until the parish boundary at Woodland Town End the road follows a series of spectacular bends between old cobble stone walls past Souterstead before dropping again by Greenrigg to Bank End and the boundary bridge over the tiny beck. This section of road has been modified and widened piecemeal to meet the needs of late 20th-century road traffic.

Before the recent rapid increase in the number of road-borne motor vehicles it was much more obvious that Torver was a small-scale route centre. The road from Coniston fanned out as it were, to give the traveller a considerable choice of destinations. There was the Ulverston road described above, and not so very different either in its line or its appearance, except that its surface was water-bound. Some of the pinnel[1] holes from which the roadmen extracted their materials may still be seen, most obviously, perhaps, next to the pinfold. Each roadman was responsible for a particular stretch of the public highway, his own 'length'. This system not only made it easier for poor maintenance to be checked, but also gave the individual workman a clearly defined responsibility. Most of the men took a great pride in 'their' section of the road, and the verges and drains were certainly better maintained then than they are today. However, the short straight section of the road up to Greystones was once a part of the Rosley Thorns fields. The earlier line of the road wound round an easier contour for horses by what is now a large lay-by. In the wall on the embankment above the new road an undated stone has been inserted, polished and pristine, still waiting after a quarter of a century for someone to come along with an inscription!

This Ulverston road had branched off from the main road – the Broughton one – over the railway bridge by the station. This bridge was demolished in the late 1960s. The Broughton road used to continue past the line of assorted cottages, ranging from the old smithy at the end of Carr Lane, to the council houses at Kitchin syke, and tortuously by the backs of Green cottages. The reason for this is that Green cottages were built, at £50 apiece, for the Furness Railway Company, which insisted that the houses must present their better side to the railway users. Then, at the southern end of the new stretch of motorway-style road, this older way, which now serves simply as a local access road, rejoins its former line. There used to be a level crossing here, and the railway house remains. The place is still known as Dalton Road crossing. This Dalton road, very narrow but with a tarmac surface, winds up between sharp-edged and menacing stone walls before emerging briefly on to the open fell above Hazel Hall. At this point a most unusual inscribed gatepost is set into the wall. It reads 'I.W. T.W. 1861' above a lozenge-shaped decorative motif. The initial refers to the Wilsons who were proprietors of Bank End and Rose Hill at that time. Then as the land falls away again below Rose Hill and Greaves Ground, the stone walls reappear, and the parish boundary is crossed near Huntpot dub (a dub is a pool in a stream) on the beck which drops down to Woodland past Haverigg Holme. From this point the road today has no hard surface, but it may be followed beyond the farm, notable for its immaculate walls, up to Climb Stile above the Woodland valley and so on for many miles to Dalton, the former market centre for Furness.

Farther along the Broughton road another very steep and narrow way leads off to the right just beyond Souterstead. This road is still used by traffic associated with the Broughton Moor quarry, and by adventurous tourists exploring the way by Appletreeworth forest to Broughton Mills. Having gained a considerable height quickly on the open fellside, the road then winds between high stone walls to Hummer bridge before leaving the parish as it begins to climb again to pass the edge of the forest above Bracelet Hall. Ultimately the road provides a line of communications either over Hoses into the lower reaches of Dunnerdale, or on beyond Duddon bridge to the Whicham valley or Millom.

To reach the upper part of the Duddon valley yet another road led out of Torver, this time from the Coniston end, at Brigg House, where another of those narrow, wall-menaced, winding roads leads past Crook and Scar Head to Tranearth, above the steep and wooded slope down to Torver beck. This road is surfaced only to Scar Head, but is passable for vehicles as far as Tranearth, now used as a base by a climbing club. Beyond Tranearth the road has to struggle as best it can past the derelict Eddy Scale quarry before joining the Walney Scar road from Coniston high up on the moor at Cove bridge. This road over the Scar was much improved during the 18th century, and for a long time was an important line of communication to Seathwaite and, if necessary, beyond. Apart from its value to industrial traffic the road was useful for men who worked at the high quarries, and socially also. Men still in middle age have tales to tell of walking back to Torver after hunt suppers or shepherds' meets, perhaps losing their lantern in one of the becks on some starless November night.

A century ago, therefore, a series of roads, each of relatively equal importance, radiated from Torver. In addition, there was a route centre within the valley, from which cartways ran out to the various quarters of the parish. This was the mill, situated in the south-eastern corner of Torver, below the magnificent falls by which Torver beck hurtles out of the vale. The falls made it easy for a water supply to be channelled to the mill which remains standing picturesquely between the falls and the mysterious stillness of the mill dub. For over 700 years all roads led to the mill, until easy long-distance communications and mass-production rendered its locally-based service obsolete. Today it is possible to trace these roads, but only on foot, so much have they already decayed. The best preserved is the road which still gives access to the occupiers of the mill, from Sunny Bank past Beckstones. Farmers from Sunny Bank, Oxen House or beyond could come with their laden pack animals or cart along this short and direct way. Another track runs steeply straight up the hillside to Emlin Hall, where the fell gate used to bar the main Ulverston road. This track is now overgrown and wet, underneath a high hedge and bank, but must once have served the farms on the western fringe of the Back Common. The most widely used of the ways to the mill was probably the third one which winds above the falls and contours round the green hillside between dykes topped with neglected hedges of ash, hazel and thorn to join Sattery lane below Moor farm. Sattery lane is still used by wheeled traffic, and continues through the flat fields in the valley bottom to reach the main road at the back of the old station yard. Everyone from the centre and north of the village would go to the mill this way, between hedgerows bedecked in their season with a wonderful profusion of wild flowers and fruits. Finally there is a fourth road from the mill, which runs up to Park Ground, and from there across to Moor. This one again is very little used now; even less so beyond Moor, where it crosses the Low Common, providing a way from Hazel Hall or Greaves Ground. Continuing farther still, it is possible to drop from Hazel Hall to the valley which slopes up on its western side to Greenrigg. All roads led to the mill, like the guiding strands running to the centre of a spider's web.

An astonishing number of old service roads criss-cross the Torver valley for there were many others, not associated with the mill, created for the convenience of farmers with business in the woodlands or out on the commons. Thus, a number of ways lead down through the woods of the Back Common to the lake shore. At Hoathwaite a cartway runs from the south-east corner of the garden, crosses a small stream and becomes more clearly defined as it passes through the formerly coppiced oak woodland, to emerge at the open space by the lake near Harrison coppice which was used for pheasant rearing in more spacious days. A similar track enters the woods hard by Grassguards. Along here folk took wood from the Back Common into the village. The way is still very plain; embanked where necessary, it passes through juniper scrub to a place where the beck is easily fordable, then descends through the wood to a point north of Moor Gill foot. Here is a wide platform above the bluff which forms the lake shore, with a stone wall along its eastern side. There are traces of piers on this wall as if it may have been a coppice barn, or at least a sheltered loading wharf for the woodland industries. The road does not continue to the bloomery site at Moor Gill foot.

Other roads wind over the High and Low Commons, for use by farmers cutting bracken or getting peat, or by persons needing to make their way to one or other of the quarries. A good example of this type of road swings at the last moment away from the mill, and crosses Torver beck by a wide ford below the mill dub. It is just discernible on the common, keeping near to the left-hand wall as one travels in a southerly direction. Then above the reservoir (usually known as Torver tarn) where the slope is steep, the track is retained on its lower side by cobbles set into the earth. This particular way eventually divides, one branch leading down by Mere beck to Sunny Bank, and the other going on over the bare common to Stable Harvey. In the old days this would be the most direct route from Stable Harvey to the mill and the rest of the village. This rough and boggy piece of common, known as Throng Moss, may also be approached by a trackway up from Hazel Hall which runs roughly in a north-easterly direction. Cuttings and embankments to ease the road round the contours of the common are visible. In several places along here are tiny tarns or very wet mosses which have the look of long disused peat cuttings. This road indeed was almost certainly a turbary track (where peat could be dug), as there is no sign of it leading to either of the bloomeries on the common. Other similar tracks lead over Birk Haw, and from the side of Poolscar wood to the desolate valley drained by the upper reaches of Mere beck, but none of them runs anywhere near the heaps of bloomery slag, either. This does seem to bear out the suggestion that the proprietors of the bloomeries were not particularly anxious to have a clearly defined approach way to the scene of their operations.

The High Common is larger than either the Low or Back Commons, and there are more ways leading over it. One road runs above the Tranearth intakes from Eddy Scale to Ash Gill quarry, then sweeps round by Bullhaw Moss back to the village at High Park. Right on the moor, above the Moss, some of the little excavations may still be seen by the roadside where stony surfacing material was obtained. This would be a quarrymen's road as much as anything; an alternative way down for people in the Greenrigg quarter of the parish forked off at the fell wall to run through the wet and stony woodland behind Undercrag. In these woods a number of charcoal burners' pitsteads may still be seen, as well as occasional mysterious little buildings which may once have sheltered the charcoal burners or bark peelers but are now no more than an uncouth scatter of rough stones. In one or two places, usually built against a wall, are the ruins of what look like stone hen-houses, which they may well have been, unless they were the ordinary residences of the once-popular gamecocks. Another important road on to the High Common ran from its farther side, beginning at Hummers. It entered the field on the north side of the main road, east of Hummer bridge and may be traced through the field and, less certainly, over Bleaberry Haws and beyond the fell wall into Seal Gill, the shallow valley between High Pike Haw and the north-western arm of the deer dyke. This would be mainly an industrial road, as it leads to the largest of the workings on the Coniston limestone outcrop.

There was, then, a whole network of communication lines within the village, for, in addition to the ones already listed, a further set of cartways or tracks connected the separate farms to the through roads and to each other. The maze of little walled ways round Low Park illustrate this point well. Many of these least-used lines of intercommunication were simply footpaths, some so seldom used as not to be clearly defined on the ground. The line of such paths may be followed from one stile to the next over the fields. One of them leaves the main Broughton road south of Brocklebank Ground formerly through a beautifully constructed gap in the wall right to the cartway which runs from Low Park to the village centre. Usually these paths cross the walls by means of three or four projecting slabs, or flags, and always, set in the wall nearby, is a hoghole for use by the sheep. If, occasionally, a path uses a gateway, it is worth examining the gateposts. There may be a stone slab at the top, with a hole through, projecting from the wall, so that a short vertical spindle set in

*Slate gate post.*

the top of the gate can slot into the hole: or there may be no gate at all. Many of the old pairs of gateposts have a line of holes pierced centrally, one above the other, like the old farmers' waistcoat buttons. The holes are square in the one post, round in the other, and were designed to accommodate roughly squared ash poles, with the thinner, still rounded ends tapering through the round ends.

Some of these footpaths and cartways must be as old as Torver itself, and long ago were as important to the inhabitants as the roads that linked them with the outside world. One of the principal duties of the Court Baron was to ensure that the ways were not blocked, or allowed to deteriorate through neglect or flooding. Later, the local Surveyor of Highways had to see to it that the major roads through the parish were kept in good order; not an onerous task when the bulk of the traffic consisted of pack animals. It was only as road maintenance became a more specialised business that responsibility for the upkeep of the highways ceased to be a local concern, and the present vast differences between the various categories of roads and pathways began to emerge. This divergence has been accentuated by the fact that by the second half of the 20th century no one needed the old ways any more.

## Chapter Sixteen

# Torver: Changing Social Structure in the 19th Century

At the beginning of the 19th century Torver was a stable, largely agricultural community, which, by the evidence of rebuilding, had gradually become more prosperous in the course of the 18th century. In the 1801 census the population was given as 182. By 1811 this figure had risen to 204, of whom 125 were chiefly employed in agriculture, and to a peak of 263 in 1821, thereafter falling to 224 in 1831 and 199 in 1841. The rise could be explained by the general fall in infant mortality rates at that time, and the subsequent decline by the greater number of these people leaving the parish when the time came for them to make their own way in the world, because there was no sudden surge of economic activity in Torver to provide work for the children of large impecunious families. James Coward is a typical, if early, illustration of the sort of thing that happened. In 1818, at the age of 14, he was bound apprentice to William Matthews, waller of Cartmel, being 'a poor child of the said township of Torver, and whose parents are not willing to maintain him'.

The increased pressure on national resources created by Napoleon's blockade has left no obvious record in the parish, although it may well be that some of the walls running up the fellsides establishing new intakes for pasture date from these years. However, the increase in population would itself explain a slightly larger scale of agricultural activity, since the extra food for fresh mouths would nearly all have to be supplied locally. The fact that the limits of cultivation had been reached, given the scope of agricultural technology at that time, links with the later decline in population. Much of this marginal land has now fallen out of cultivation, and only the decaying walls remain, for example, on the heathland above Torver Park, and beyond Tranearth.

Although in general Torver has always been sparsely documented, there are several snapshots of the changing social structure in the 19th century to be found in the commercial directories which were a feature of the period. None of these gives full details of the parish, but each does indicate what were thought to be important occupations, and who were considered (or considered themselves) as the most significant personages. The Parson and White Directory of 1829 is the earliest. It reflects a pre-industrial, pre-railway world, and could easily refer to 1779. There is only one 'gentleman' in the person of Mr. J. Sanders of Hoathwaite; not, historically, the premier dwelling of Torver, nor an ancient name in the locality. There are 10 yeomen and nine other farmers. Whilst some of the yeomen lived at the larger farms, such as High Stile and Undercrag, others lived in little places now ruined, like Garth Nook and Grassguards. By contrast, Anthony Smith of Souterstead and A. Fleming of Brackenbarrow, two of the most important and ancient settlements in the village, are listed as plain 'farmers'. There is continuing evidence of how, as in the 18th century, two families shared the same address. Thus, Thomas Kendall, farmer, lived at Hoathwaite, probably in the older house now used for animals and storage, across the yard from Mr. Sanders's more modern and commodious dwelling, enlarged during the previous century. Robert Woodend farmed at Grassguards. His cottage was so small that its ruins are difficult to decipher, and his land holding must have been tiny. These men and their families constituted the backbone of the community. Michael, in Wordsworth's poem, gives a vivid picture of their everyday lives and their outlook, but they themselves have left no memorial.

The Directory records a few other people. John Briggs of Park Ground acted as a carrier. He departed for Ulverston at 4 a.m. on Thursdays (market day), arriving 'evening'. Presumably this means arriving back at Torver. However bad the roads or poor the horses, such an early start would leave plenty of time for the round 22 mile trip, with an interval for business and refreshment whilst in town. John Briggs was really a farmer who did some spare time carrying. The same sort of thing might be said, no doubt unkindly, of Matthew Carter the curate, who at that time farmed Rosley Thorns. Robert Fleming, currently the miller ('corn miller'), would come nearer to being able to live independently of farming, as would Jude Breade of Church House, who was a blacksmith. Like J. Cookson of Hollows, a shoemaker, each of these men was able to meet a particular need which was most conveniently met by someone who was to hand locally. All this is just as it had been in the early years of the 18th century. Many other needs could await the next call by a pedlar, or the opportunity of a visit, perhaps by a neighbour, to Ulverston. There are only two men whose occupation puts them right outside the circle of full time farmers: Edward Park Jnr., the schoolmaster, whose father farmed Undercrag, and John Atkinson, the owner of Ash Gill slate quarry. Basically therefore, this is still Torver as it had been since the earliest days when the first settlers created homesteads for themselves by clearing the original forest.

But it was not long after 1829 that changes of an entirely new kind began to make themselves felt, changes brought about by the industrial revolution and a vastly improved transport system. The Mannex Directory of 1849 begins to reflect some of these changes. The hungry cotton mills of South Lancashire required millions of wooden bobbins, and the people who worked in the mills needed pills when they were unwell. The woodlands of High Furness were able to supply both bobbins for the mills and boxes for the pills, and Torver beck hurls itself down by Sunny Bank with enough force to operate a big wheel. So it is not surprising to find here in 1849 Wilson Brunskill, bobbin maufacturer, and William Kendall, pill box maker. The increasing specialisation implicit in the overall development of the national economy shows in a tiny way by the inclusion of Thomas Crewdson, joiner.

By 1850 there was perceptibly more travelling than in the past, with more folk passing through the parish, even as tourists, and more men were employed in the quarries, which were now sending their products to a wider market. Within the decade the railway had even penetrated beyond Torver to Coniston. It may be the presence of travellers and thirsty quarrymen who account for the fact that John Wilson (Wilson Cottages) combined his blacksmithing with keeping a beerhouse. In addition, there was Thomas Massicks, host at the *Church House*, just across the way. Massicks induced some ravings from the rambling A. C. Gibson (*Ramblings and Ravings*, 1849), who was more impressed by the house than by the church adjoining,

'A snug and tidy public house, known pretty widely by the title of Torver Kirkhouse, and if you happen to be athirst, I can honestly recommend Thomas Massick's home-brewed ale'. Gibson, after commenting on the 'old, but comfortable and substantial dwellings', and the 'remarkably verdant fields', took the road which 'the guide post tells you leads to Ulverston – if you can't read, ask at the blacksmith's shop'. He does not say whether he took this further opportunity of assuaging his thirst.

To return to the Mannex Directory. Nearly all the entries are 'farmers', 21 of them, of whom seven are described as 'owners'. These comprise George Park of Undercrag, John Park of Brocklebank Ground, John Parker of Hazel Hall, William Wilson of High Stile, and Matthew Towers and Daniel Birkett of 'Cragg', this being the name formerly given to the thickly populated area comprising Torver Park and Scar Head. Crag was also the address of John Biggins, farmer. The principal landowners were Mr. Sanders, whom we met at Hoathwaite in 1829, Mr. Park of Brocklebank Ground, and Mrs. B. Brocklebank. There had not therefore been any significant movement towards the establishment of a squirearchy since 1829. The changes had been mainly small ones, which we can now see as pointers to the future, such as the larger scale of activity at Sunny Bank, and the arrival of the thirsty Mr. Gibson.

The 1851 Census return for Torver fills out the picture shown in the directories. Some of the agricultural holdings were very small. William Robinson, farmer, of Greenrigg, held three acres, as did Matthew Towers at Low Park. Others combined farming with some additional occupation, like John Wilson of Carr Cottage. He farmed four acres, kept a beerhouse and was the village blacksmith. William Smith mixed farming with shoemaking. Farm work was, of course, the principal activity, and accounted for the occupation of 28 of the 41 households listed, with a designation ranging from 'agricultural labourer' to 'landed proprietor'. The other occupations listed reflect the industries which were flourishing throughout High Furness at this period. Wood-turning was not confined to William Kendal's large establishment at Sunny Bank; William Danson of Bridge House also followed this craft. One man was a slate river, another a copper miner. The considerable increase in carting which growing industrial activity must have involved provided work for Thomas Crewdson of Church House, cart- and wheel-wright. An unusual business was that of John Biggins and his son at High Park. They were described as 'calker-makers'. Calkers are pointed pieces on horseshoes placed so as to prevent slipping; no doubt in regular demand at a time when so many horses would be working up and down the steep and slippery ways over the moors to the mines and quarries. Numbers of horses were also employed inside the Coniston copper mines to haul out wagon-loads of ore, a situation again in which calkers would give the animal a better grip where the surface was wet and uneven. Calkers nevertheless formed only a part of John Biggins' stock-in-trade: the 1866 Mannex Directory describes him prosaically as 'clog-iron maker'.

At Hollace, where William Butler the schoolmaster lodged (he was aged 44 and hailed from Gosforth in West Cumberland), James Dockrey carried on the trade of shoemaker. This house had a long association with shoemaking – J. Cookson had worked there in 1829. William Smith was also a shoemaker, living at Grassguards where he employed an apprentice, so maybe Torver footwear was a Furness speciality in the mid-19th century. The remaining listed occupations are the traditional ones. The parson was then living at Souterstead, Thomas Massicks of Church House was the innkeeper, and Moses Harrison the miller. Almost everyone above the grade of agricultural labourer kept at least one servant, and one or two folk were able to live quite comfortably – Daniel Birkett of Scar Head, landed proprietor of 10 acres, maintained a household of two servants, and at Hoathwaite Thomas Saunders, gentleman, originally from Derbyshire, left the farm work to Henry Hudson and his family. However, a circumstance which bears out Martineau's rather dismal picture of the village at this period is that 10 houses were uninhabited.

Then, the opening of the Furness Railway in 1859 gave an immediate impetus to industry by making it much easier to send slate further afield; in the longer run it did more than any other single factor to break down the old isolation. The farmer could get his beasts to Broughton market more easily; the householder could seriously consider working at Millom or Barrow where the new iron industry was growing; all kinds of domestic and agricultural equipment were now more readily obtainable. Quite apart from the obvious way in which new jobs were created – stationmaster, platelayer or engine crew – the importance of the railway to the community may be deduced from the frequency with which it came to figure in the deliberations of the vestry and, later, the parish meeting.

The 1882 Mannex Directory gives us the chance to look at Torver again after a further generation's movement towards greater specialisation of activities. The railway and post office had both become established elements in the local scene. David Sykes Walker was the stationmaster, and a little way along the line towards Woodland lived John Brockbank the platelayer, at Dalton Road House, by the level crossing where the old road to Dalton turned onto the fellside. Myles Jackson, blacksmith as well as postmaster, would see to it that your letters were promptly despatched at 1.00 p.m., and when the messenger arrived from Coniston at 9.30 a.m. with the incoming mail, he would be there also.

The bobbin mill had extended the range of its products, partly to meet local demand, for this was the great age of the Coniston copper mines, and now included pick- and hammer shafts. Richard Charnley was the proprietor and Leonard Clark of Elm How is also listed as a pick- and hammer shaft maker. There were two joiners-cum-wheelwrights, Thomas Jackson of Souterstead and Richard Clark of Church House, eking out his victualling by this means. All this represents a wider variety of industrial and commercial enterprise than ever before. Many more carts than formerly must have been in use at this time, for bringing down slate from Ash Gill, Goldscope and Eddy Scale; for leading timber and other products from the woodlands; for fetching peats from the mosses, as well as for the other immemorial uses of the farmers. Mary Fleming of Scarhead is listed in the Directory as 'cart-owner'.

In 1882 industry was further represented by Joseph Jackson, slate merchant, of High Torver Park, and John Wilson, basket maker, of Greenrigg. These two exemplify the basic natural resources of the area, slate and timber, being exploited on a larger scale than ever before. The baskets were known as swills, made of oak strips called spales and a rim or bool of hazel. There was another swill shop just below Scarhead not listed in 1882, but the remains of which were still visible in 1970. The baskets were widely distributed, for example to Liverpool, where the big shipping lines found them ideal for men to carry when loading coal at those exotic bunkering stations, such as Aden. In 1882 the self sufficiency of the ancient community was dented for the first time by the inclusion of shopkeepers – Mary Coulthard, grocer, of Ellishow Cottage (next to Hollace) and Samuel Crabtree. Their establishments were very reminiscent of the one briefly managed by Ginger and Pickles in Beatrix Potter's immortal story. Also, Robert Jones kept the *Car Cottage Inn* as a beerhouse. There is reason to suppose that this is the same place as the one which Gibson knew, and that it was subsequently known as the *Miners Arms.*

*Swill basket.*

If we could be transported back to 1882, we should not find it all that strange, for there had been more changes in the previous 30 years than in any comparable period before. But the backbone of the community was still its agriculture. The land was chiefly pasture, 'stock rearing and butter making being the farmers' chief employment'. There was not now an overriding necessity for a man to grow his own grain, and so the acreage of land under the plough had declined by comparison with former days. The Board of Agriculture statistics for 1905 give 97 acres arable, 1,161 acres permanent grass and 111 acres woods and plantations. The principal landowners still included the Parks of Brocklebank Ground, along with Mrs. Barratt of Coniston and Mary Wilson, whose estates comprised Bank End, Rose Hill and Town End (Woodland) to make a compact unit at the southern extremity of the village. Two farmers are described also as 'carters': William Charnley of Scar Head and Thomas Wilson of 'Trenwith' (Tranearth). Both these farmers were well placed to take advantage of the comings and goings from the quarries, as well as along the road over Walna Scar into Dunnerdale.

An unmistakable feeling of greater prosperity pervades this 1882 Directory. It was the high noon of the Rev. Thomas Ellwood's long and fruitful incumbency which had begun so auspiciously on that sunny summer day in 1861 when the whole valley had seemed to sing for him. The dignified rectory had recently been completed and the second rebuilding of the church was in train. The old Baptist chapel at Sunny Bank had been re-roofed on the initiative of John Birkett, whose family had a long history of association with nonconformity in the parish. Three quarries were being worked on the moor, and the woodland-based industries, charcoal burning, basket making and tanning, were thriving. And there was now rather more than a bare minimum of folk outside the basic farming circle, represented in 1849 only by the parson and the schoolmaster.

In the later years of the 19th century Torver reached the highest point of its prosperity and social development, although the population remained steady at about the 200 mark. The second edition of Bulmer's Directory, dating from just before the First World War, enables us to look back on this golden afternoon of steam age civilisation. In the 1831 census we read that 27 of the 66 men aged over 20 were employed in agriculture; of the 15 connected with retail trade and handicraft, most were involved in woodland industries, as together with quarrying, would be the 16 labourers (non agricultural). Some of these men would almost certainly work in agriculture part-time, as numbers of village men do today, although they would not give farm work as their occupation. Only four men came into the category which included 'clergy, capitalists, professional and other educated men'. Eighty years later agriculture was still the largest single industry, but the other categories were much more varied, and the 'educated men' were making a rather better showing.

There were still no country squires; the person nearest to this kind of position was Mr. J. W. H. Barratt, and he lived in Coniston. Significantly, the rural councillor was one of the statesmen-farmers, whose Torver lineage extended back over many generations, William Wilson of High Stile. The stability of the social milieu is further indicated by the continuing presence of the Wilsons from Bank End and the Parks of Brocklebank Ground in the list of landowners. Many of the inhabitants, says the editor of the Directory, 'find employment in the manufacture of oak baskets, hammer shafts, etc. at Sunny Bank and Greenrigg'. But there was also a considerable number of people in the parish engaged in specialised and responsible work. Torver station now boasted a post and telegraph office. Thomas Wilson, the postmaster, would issue and cash postal orders, and then walk or cycle back to Bank End after dealing with the 5.25 p.m. dispatch of mail. Since 1882 Torver had also risen in the railway hierarchy. The current tenant of the house at Dalton Road Crossing was John Thomas Coward, a 'foreman platelayer'. The Rev. R. D. Ellwood was assisting his father, now a very old man, and acting as secretary of the Institute. The school, too, was flourishing as never before. The master was Henry Bullock, who lived at the Larches, Souterstead, and he had an assistant, Miss Hannah Barrow. Then, at Scar Head, in case any of the Torver youngsters should show a rebellious disposition to truancy, lived the School Attendance Officer, Mr. John Lindsay. Mr. George Harrison, a solicitor, lived at Beckstones, and at Brigg House Mr. A. H. Riggmaiden, now remembered for the small charity which bears his name, so that around the turn of the century there was a large enough number of persons in the 'educated' category to form the nucleus of a social circle.

Bulmer also records a greater variety of business establishments, although not R. W. Prickett's grocery store at 'Ells Howe', which had certainly been in existence in 1903, successor to Mary Coulthard, and remained until 1979, by which time it had long been Torver's only shop. George Wilford of Souterstead was a fish and fruit dealer. Presumably he travelled round the area with horse and cart, taking his goods to his customers, providing a valuable service in so scattered a community. At No. 11 Green Cottages Mrs. W. Dixon kept a baker's shop. The alternative to the *Church House* for a convivial evening was no longer known as the *Car Cottage Inn*, but as Mrs. Mary Casson's *Miner's Arms*, a name which suggests the work place of many of the local men and their cronies, as well as recalling the shade of Mistress Quickly.

These directories are not exhaustive. More detailed work with parish registers, for example, might cause some of the suggestions made above to be modified. But the picture would remain, of a stable community adapting itself to the new strains and pressures created by the industrialisation of 19th-century England, becoming more varied and more broadly based in the process, but never losing its social cohesion or its identity, and participating eventually in the gradual rise in living standards which followed the first catastrophic impact of the factories.

## A typical Directory entry for Torver

### 1866 Mannex Directory: Torver Township

Letters arrive through Church Coniston
John Biggins: clog-iron maker
Wilson Brunskill: bobbin-turner
Miss Jane Braithwaite
Mr. John Birkett
Rev. Thomas Ellwood: Incumbent
William Coward: miller
Moses Harrison: corn miller
Coniston Slate Co.: slate quarry masters
Miles Jackson: blacksmith
J. Knight: schoolmaster
Mary Lindow: Beerhouse
Jane Massicks: vict., Church House
Mr. Edward Park: Torver Park
Edward Steel: shoemaker and postmaster
Thomas Walton: grocer and parish clerk
David S. Walker: Stationmaster

*Farmers: y = yeoman.*
Joseph Barrow, Howthwaite
Thomas Barrow, Park Ground

John Birkett
John Bell
Thos. Briggs (& carrier to Ulverston)
Richard Crook
Nicholas Gibson
Moses Harrison y
James Lambert
Edward Park y Brocklebank Ground
George Park y
Elizabeth Parker, Hazel Hall
Edward Parker
Richard Prickett, Crook Farm
Anthony Smith y
Daniel Tyson
Isaac Tyson
Thomas Walter
Thomas Wilson y
William Wilson y

## Chapter Seventeen

# Twentieth-Century Torver

In the first decade of the 20th century, then, the prospects for the future of the village must have looked brighter than ever before. Best of all, the school was bursting at the seams, and the talk was all of raising money to enlarge the building so that the master and his assistant could each work in a separate and reasonably-sized room. This ambition was to be realised when the Bishop of Carlisle came on 28 November 1914 to open the additions, and everyone sang again the hymn that Mr. Ellwood had composed specially for the opening of the new school in 1873:

> Bless our work at length completed,
> Bless the children gathering here,
> On Thy throne of mercy seated
> To their prayer still lend an ear ...

Education was a thing that Torver folk believed in; most of them anyway. Not many years back it had been suggested that the income from the Fleming School Charity should be apportioned in relief of rates, but under the leadership of the rector, there was a 5:2 majority at the parish meeting for the motion that the income should be used to fund a scholarship tenable at a secondary school, and only go in relief of rates if not claimed in any given year. Also, there was a Technical Instruction Committee which dealt with the Reading Room, housed in the tiny, rather ramshackle building that doubled as the village Institute, situated in the field opposite the present bus shelter. (It was sold in 1926 for £6.) This committee had come into being as early as 1892, when on 15 October there was a lively debate at the vestry meeting. They were considering the question of technical instruction, and some wanted to have a woodcarving class. Encouraged by the approbation of Professor Ruskin, this was a very popular and harmless hobby to occupy the men at that time – in Coniston so many people carved that they even erected a long, narrow 'carving house' on the end of the Institute. But another faction demanded a class in veterinary science, perhaps feeling that a little more knowledge in this direction could not fail to be useful to members of an agricultural community. When Ellwood, inevitably chairman of the meeting, gave his casting vote to woodcarving, there was such an uproar that they decided to reconsider the whole question at a meeting open to all ratepayers. It was at this meeting, held on 1 November, that the Technical Instruction Committee was formed, and a majority voted for veterinary science. By now, unfortunately, Mr. Kendall of Barrow, the first choice as lecturer, had made other arrangements, so they had to make do with an otherwise unidentified Mr. Glaister.

The main preoccupation of the parish meetings in the early part of the 20th century was with the roads, and other means of communication. Almost the first act of the parish meeting after its formation in 1894 was to ask the Highways Board for a snow plough not less than six feet wide. This was a wedge-shaped, horse-propelled contrivance which had to be brought into service each winter. They kept a close eye on the Furness Railway Company as well. In 1898 a sharp note was sent when the Company withdrew trucking facilities for cattle and sheep at the station. This meant that the farmers had to carry (or walk) stock at an early hour to Coniston or Woodland for the market train to Broughton. Six months later a resolution followed, thanking the Company for providing a cattle siding at Torver. In fact, the cattle were now better provided for than the people. There was neither a bell at the office in the goods yard to attract the attention of the stationmaster to the presence of persons with horses having business there, nor a ladies' closet at the station proper. These two deficiencies were pointed out on 31 March 1909, and after two years the Company got round to installing a bell, but still no waiting room or conveniences for the ladies. The post office also came in for its share of badgering, especially on the question of Sunday collections and deliveries of mail, generally considered to be inadequate. The parish meeting was quite prepared to be specific in its demands: why not, they asked in March 1913, have letter boxes at Sunny Bank and Greenrigg, and have a portable box at the station to go on the 6.39 train to Foxfield, where it could join the mail train? Why not, indeed? By August of the same year, they were thanking the Postmaster General for attending to this.

The proprietors of Eddy Scale quarry, however, were much less amenable. Every few years the clerk would write to Messrs. Mandalls about their dangerous activities, sometimes invoking the name of the county council, but always, it seems, in vain. In 1897 the public right of way to Seathwaite by Eddy Scale had been 'stopped'. In 1902 it was 'obstructed', to such a degree that 'the highway is illegally diverted and is now dangerous through the spoil bank overhanging the road'. In 1903 they tried to bring in the Commissioner of Woods and Forests, on the grounds that 'stone from the spoil bank at Addy Scale was carried down Torver Beck to the damage of land adjoining the said bank'. Mandalls remained obdurately inactive. The same point was raised in 1921 and again in 1935. Today the quarry has long been derelict, and the road is still 'dangerous'; the spoil bank looms menacingly and the wall leans inwards at an extraordinary angle.

The abandoned quarries – Casson Brockbank sleeping at Ash Gill in a rough shelter, exchanging messages with the men on their long trek to work at Broughton Moor, Eddy Scale left to the foxes and the wheatears – give the clue to what has happened to the secure, rather cosy picture of Torver as it was in the first decade of the 20th century. Yet, superficially, in the 1920s, the scene had not changed much. There was little except purely local traffic on the bumpy roads, which reflected the prevailing weather by their dusty or muddy condition. The young Barr boys would sometimes station themselves at the fell gate by Emlin Hall in hopes of earning an honest copper, but most of the traffic went by rail. There were a dozen trains a day between Coniston and Foxfield, starting with the 6 a.m. workmen's train. By contrast, the road carrier, Joseph Jackson of Water Yeat, came from Blawith to Coniston twice weekly with his horse-drawn, two-wheeled covered waggon. Mr. Bob Woodburn of Town Mill Ulverston would call on people for orders once a month. The goods would be delivered to Torver station the following week, and Richard Prickett would cart them round to their several destinations. Once a month a two-horse tank waggon would bring paraffin and petrol from Ulverston to be put, usually, into two-gallon tins. Weekly rounds were made by 'Butcher Barrow' of Gateside, Coniston, with his horse-drawn van, and by a Flookburgh man selling fruit and vegetables from a flat cart drawn by a pony. Then respectful little Mr. Woods, the manager of Coniston Co-operative Society, would come for orders once a month. The ensuing delivery could easily be a major event in the domestic calendar, with the unloading of flour in sacks, and drums of paraffin oil, kept well apart one hopes, in the delivery cart. To lend a little variety to the road transport scene, Mr. Edwards the postman, and the district nurse would make their rounds on bicycles; Dr. Kendall always came from Coniston on horseback.

Superficially, too, the old self-sufficiency of the community was scarcely dented in the mid-1920s. At this time Mr. J. C. Appleyard had a new house built for himself and his wife, which he named 'Greystones'. The house was planned by Mr. and Mrs. Appleyard in consultation with local tradesmen, without benefit of advice from any professional architect. Mr. J. J. Satterthwaite of Nibthwaite sawmill did the joinery, Messrs. Leck and Carter of Lowick the building, and Mr. A. Taylor of Greenodd the plumbing. The slate came from Eddy Scale quarry, some of the stone from a tiny quarry above Kelly Hall on the adjacent Back Common, and the wood for the downstairs floors from the old airship shed at Walney. Also in the '20s, Mr. Jock Wilson was still making swills in his shop at Scar Head. On Mondays he would boil his wood in the big iron trough that was rusted and decayed by the '60s. This was one of the dirtiest jobs imaginable, as the tannin came out of the wood and splashed over everything as he reached the pieces from their hot bath. For the rest of the week he would be sitting in the corner apartment of his premises on his mare, working away at his baskets. The swiller sits astride one end of this mare, placing the long thin piece of split wood, known as a 'tarr', before him, and anchoring it down by a primitive-looking but effective pedal-operated wooden brake block. Then, taking his two-handled drawknife, rather resembling an outsize spokeshave, he draws the blade towards himself, smoothing the tarr so that it is ready to be woven in and out as part of the body of a basket. And as Jock Wilson worked, in the woods behind the village, and over on the east side of the lake, the smoke from the charcoal burners' fires would rise into the autumn air.

The farmers, too, lived much as their ancestors had done. There was some horse-drawn machinery, and George Barr at Moor was something of a phenomenon, because he whizzed round his hayfields in a converted motor, with someone else sitting on the cutter, or whatever it may have been, to manipulate its controls. Haymaking, and even more, clipping, were busy times of the farming year, when neighbours all lent each other a helping hand. At clipping there was a job for everyone, just as there was at haytime. The children would be handy to pass the salve if someone had slightly misjudged his shears, or to roll up a shorn fleece, or bring refreshment out to the men. The occasion would end happily with music and dancing on the empty barn floor.

There was still a wide variety of small and specialised buildings about the farm – a stable with storage space above, perhaps for seed hay; a cart house, often of timber-framed construction and open on one or two sides to house the plough, the harrow, the roller and the multitude of hand implements as well as the sled and/or cart; a cow house (shuppon) for the small number of milk cows; an adjacent calf

*Sheep shearing bench, clippers, horn cup and wooden bowl of 'smit' or 'salve' for marking sheep.*

house (hull, hole); an outbarn for the stirks (yearling cows); even farther out, right in the fields, a hoghouse to shelter the sheep, which had to take their chance out of doors in all weathers, and were fed the poorer, leafy hay into the bargain, when they got anything at all. Then there was a pig hole, usually at the back of the farm, and a hen house. Sometimes there might be a line of bee-boles along a sheltered sunny wall. Geese were smitted just like lambs with their owner's mark, and turned out on the rough land to graze. it was said that the foxes were less likely to take an animal that had been smitted, perhaps because of the smell of the tar, or on account of the residual human odour. In any event, there were fewer foxes in those days, no doubt because of the more widespread activity on the commons.

Sheep or store cattle for market were usually walked to Broughton along the road that until the late 1940s was little more than a country lane overarched with trees. The eclipse of the railway is presaged in the neglect of that trucking facility for which they had shouted so loudly in 1898. Every farmer grew some oats, more rarely wheat or flax, and visited the still-working mills at Lowick or Broughton Mills. The arable land would also carry a crop of turnips to go into the turnip hole as winter feed for stock, and potatoes as winter feed for humans. In the autumn the farmer would take his ley (scythe) to cut brackens from the fell, and not only to go into the bracken store as winter bedding for his animals. There were still houses with bracken on their floors in the Torver of the 1920s. Although it was now easy enough to obtain coal from the railway station, it was nevertheless cheaper to work the peat mosses and bring down the cut peats to be stacked in the peat house, using a small and narrow horse-drawn sledge.

Sheep remained the basis of the agricultural economy, as they had always been. Each farm had the right to turn a certain number of sheep on to the fell – the specified number is known as a man's 'grassing'. In the old days the sheep were more often Herdwicks or of doubtful ancestry, than today, and were much wilder than they are now, so that gathering could be a really difficult job. The Shepherds' Meet continued to flourish because it filled a very real need for everyone using the wide grazing area of the high fells. The Walna Scar Shepherds' Meet met every year at Walna Scar quarry in mid-July. This quarry is situated on the Seathwaite side of the pass, and is a convenient point for a lot of men and dogs to assemble with whatever stray sheep they have acquired since the previous meet. Normally they know well enough to whom the strays belong, by the distinguishing clips and holes in the animals' ears. These marks are all listed in the old flock book which each farmer possesses. As well as bringing these sheep, the farmers also brought quantities of food and ale, because it is a long and thirsty walk to this remote place, and in mid-July there was no need to hurry back. The Valley meeting and dinner take place in early November on a rotation between the *Newfield* at Seathwaite, the *Blacksmith's Arms* at Broughton Mills and the Torver *Church House*. This November meeting is now enlivened by a show of sheep, dogs and sticks, by a fell race or a hound trail, and by singing competitions. Some years ago, the dinner and the post-prandial drinking songs were the chief attraction of this important social occasion, the origin of which is lost in antiquity. Certainly it has always been fully supported by the farmers in the area under consideration, which comprises Seathwaite, Dunnerdale, Broughton, Woodland, Torver and Coniston. To pick a date at random, 1937, the names of the officers for that year show the standing of the Meet in the esteem of the farming community by the respect in which they were universally held: Chairman, W. H. Tyson, Broughton Mills; Treasurer, S. Inman, Spoon Hall (Coniston); Secretary, G. T. Hartley, Turner Hall (Seathwaite).

*Bygone shepherds' 'tools of the trade'.*

Fewer people attended the Meets in the late 1970s simply because there were fewer farmers. It is not that farming has declined as an industry; the number of separate farming units has diminished drastically, although several folk keep a few sheep or cattle as a part-time occupation. Other industries have declined to the point of complete disappearance. The woodland industries had petered out by the 1930s; the Torver quarries withered as those on either side of the parish expanded; and as road communications became so cheap and easy after the mid-20th century, the railway became less and less essential to the local economy. Although the parish meeting protested vigorously about the proposed closure in 1957, as recently as the previous year there had been agitation for a bus to replace the train for transporting pupils to Coniston school, on grounds, principally it seems, of safety. Evidently some of the children had been experimenting with the carriage doors at various unsuitable points along the route.

By 1957 the schoolchildren had been going into Coniston for 30 years. The last manager to be appointed to Torver school by the parish council, to keep an eye on the last rites, had been Mr. R. Boyren in 1928. Why the school should have been closed at precisely this point is not clear. At the 1931 census the population of the village was 196 as compared with 184 in 1911, when the school seemed to be booming, and there were 52 families as against forty-one. Presumably the Lancashire Education Committee could see no future in the long term for such a small school, and had decided to concentrate resources with a wider range of equipment and facilities at Coniston.

Certainly, this long-term forecast was the correct one. The history of the past 40 years seems to consist of nothing but a catalogue of decline, spiritual as well as economic. The Baptist chapel at Sunny Bank struggled on into the 1940s, when even the occasional token services that had maintained a thread of continuity, were discontinued. The building was later bought by the owner of Sunny Bank farm, and now stands sad and empty, overshadowed by the trees that have grown up round it. No trace remains of the wooden steps that used to lead into the little round baptismal pond on the open fellside outside the chapel wall. The parish church celebrated its jubilee as St Luke's in 1934, but the general gradual decline in the habit of churchgoing has not been offset, as in Coniston, by the presence of holidaymaking worshippers. The church has not benefited, either, from being incorporated with Coniston for pastoral purposes. The ancient distribution of charity monies was discontinued in the early 1960s, but in 1978 the Fleming Schoolmaster Charity was resurrected after a lapse of a generation to help 16-year old Torver leavers from the secondary school in Coniston.

On the economic side, and also at Sunny Bank, Charnley's mill gradually reduced its output in the 1930s, and limited the range of its products until its closure shortly before the start of the Second World War. By 1960 such activities as swill basket making and charcoal burning existed only in the memories of the older folk. Even the presence of the military, who protected George Constantinesco's[1] important researches at Oxen House, and who made extensive use of the commons for firing practice during the 1940s, did nothing to arrest the economic decline. They simply travelled in every day, and by their activities created many an exciting diversion for the local boys, incidentally making a dreadful mess of the road past Tranearth.

The causes of decay in Torver are those which have affected rural life in general since the era of mass-production and the motor car became firmly established. Yet to write of decay and to praise the old days is altogether too simplistic. Standards of living are far higher than at any time in the past, and the loss of social amenities and shopping facilities within the village has been compensated for the majority with access to their own means of transport, by the ease of getting to a much wider range of functions and shops elsewhere. The minority who do not own a car, by contrast, are more effectively imprisoned within a largely sterile environment than their ancestors for many generations. The decline of traditional industries, moreover, has been counterbalanced to some extent by the development of new ones. There is no village blacksmith, perhaps, but there is a flourishing garage, known throughout the north of England for its expertise in that specialised branch of the car industry based on the Landrover. The farmers no longer do weaving, or a bit of work in the woodlands, but many of the residents, not only farmers, are involved in the tourist industry, and cater for visitors either by directly providing accommodation or by permitting a limited amount of camping or caravan parking.

These newer industries, however, are not integrally linked with the local economy as were the older ones, and do not provide the same base for purely local employment. To a greater extent than ever in the past, persons who live in Torver work elsewhere, and a greater number of properties than ever before languish in the ownership of folk who use them merely as second homes or for letting to holidaymakers. By contrast with 1911 there is now no pastor, no schoolmaster, no stationmaster and no postmaster. The changes of the past half century have been greater and more rapid than at any time in the past, so that the historian is made aware more of the present discontinuity than of the long preceding centuries of slowly-evolving tradition.

*Appendix One*

# Select Glossary of Torver Place Names

## TORVER:

*Thorverga* in a charter of Gilbert Fitzreinfred, dated before 1220, and quoted by W. G. Collingwood.
*Thorvergh* in Assize rolls, 1246.
*Torvergh* in Inquest taken at Ulverston in 1316.
The second element looks like -ergh, a clearing in O.N.; the first element has puzzled students of language. One can choose, with Ekwall, 'where turves are cut' – utilitarian, or 'belonging to Thor' – romantic. After all, the old name for Coniston Water is Thurstan (Thorstein) Mere.

## GREAVES GROUND

*Gravs Ground* 1698. The obvious possibility here is a personal name, linked with 'Ground'. This is a very common type of place name in High Furness – cf. Atkinson Ground in Coniston, or Brocklebank Ground in Torver itself. These names usually date from the end of the Middle Ages when a person was given permission by the lord of the manor to fence off a compact piece of land from the manorial 'waste' for cultivation. Unfortunately, Graves was not a Torver name. The other possibility is that 'Gravs' was originally a title. The word 'grave' was formerly used, as in 'moltergrave', with reference to the miller, to mean an executive officer; so maybe this was where the lord's manorial steward used to live.

## STEERS POOL

This is part of the boundary between Torver and Woodland, below Greaves Ground. Steers may be a personal name, 'Styr's'. It is interesting principally as illustrating the use of the word 'pool' to mean a stream, cf. Rusland Pool which drains the Rusland valley.

## GARTH NOOK

*Garth Nooke* 1706. Garth is O.N., meaning enclosed ground, garden, paddock, and a nook is a secluded place. This site, near Hazel Hall, looking out over Woodland, and sheltered by the wooded slopes behind, must have been quite a comfortable little corner.

## HAZEL HALL

*Hessel How* 1606. In O.S., hesli means hazel. Hazels have long been common hereabouts, and formed the principal constituent of the old coppice woodland. It is not certain which of the occupiers first dignified the status of the residence at no financial cost by converting How (O.S., low hill) into Hall.

## MOOR
*More* 1599, when 'John of the More' was mentioned in the parish register. This is an apt name – from the farmyard you look on to land only precariously held under cultivation. A few years of neglect, and all would be 'more' again.

## MERE BECK
In O.E. 'maere' means a boundary. The stream forms the boundary between Torver and Blawith before joining Torver beck by Sunny Bank. There also used to be the mere stones, marking off individual sections in the town field by Torver beck, below the pinfold. Ellwood (*Landnama Book of Iceland*, 1894) says that until 1893 three mere stones were to be seen in this field. Then in 1893 the three adjoining ownerships were merged into one.

## STABLE HARVEY
*Stabel Hervy* 1291 (quoted in A. P. Brydson, *Two lakeland Townships*).
*Stabilherin* 1314. This is a real puzzle, unless the obvious and simple explanation really is the correct one. After all, by the time a string of packhorses had reached this remote spot, they and the packmen would be ready for a rest and a bit of bait. The old packway from down the Crake valley used to run by Stable Harvey and over the Low Common to Torver village and beyond. Or again, we may wonder whether William de Lancaster kept horses here for the convenience of his occasional hunting parties.

## OXEN HOUSE
*Oxenous* 1599, *Oxenhus* 1612. This does look like oxen & house. The word oxen was regularly used, cf. the inventory of John Chamley 1697.

## SUNNY BANK
This name is self-explanatory and fully justified. The farm is on a south-facing slope looking towards the foot of Coniston Water.

## BECKSTONES
This is another descriptive name. 'Beck' is used almost universally for 'stream' in this area. It may not be fanciful to suggest that cobbles from nearby Torver beck were used in the construction of the earliest dwelling on the site. Rounded, undressed cobble-stones were certainly widely used in local building work until quite recent times.

## DILLICARS
Allis Deliker, died 1599.
Margaret, wife of William Dilicker, died 1641.
Dillicars, or Delicars, consists of six small walled fields grouped in a roughly circular shape round a central hub, in which are the undecipherable ruins of a small building. The fields have been enclosed from the Back Common on the east-facing slope above Sunny Bank chapel. Ellwood, with his wide knowledge of Scandinavian languages, suggested 'carr', meaning a rather marshy piece of wood or field, and 'deeal', corresponding to the Icelandic 'deila', meaning to divide. Here we have an area enclosed from the common and divided into small fields. One wonders whether,

originally, the ownership of these fields changed annually, in rotation, like the strips in the town field. This is not totally convincing, but more satisfactory than explanations involving Furness monks and dill plantations, etc.

## EMLIN HALL
*Em How* 1599, *Em Hous* 1615, *Elm Hall* 1771. This looks like another case of the Hazel Hall social upgrading process, but 'Em' is less obvious than 'Hessel'. An O.E. word, 'emm', means 'smooth', which would make descriptive sense, geographically, with the 'how'. The elms of 1771 are probably as imaginary as the hall and were equally created by the Biglands who lived there at the time.

## ROSLEY THORNS
*Roselay Thornes* 1599. This name is not likely to have any connexion with roses. The O.S. 'hross', meaning horse, could give the first element, and in O.N. 'leah' means a glade, or open space in woodland. But there is no documentary evidence earlier than 1599, and so no means of knowing whether the place had any connexion with Stable Harvey across the valley.

## HOLLACE
*Hollas* 1599, *Hollhouse* 1714, *Holowhouse* 1719. Fitting snugly into the side of a tiny dry valley overlooking the town field, 'house in the hollow' would be a very suitable name for this farmstead.

## HIGH STILE
*Hie Stele* 1585. In O.E. 'stele' means ridge or precipice. Precipice exaggerates somewhat, but this farm is situated high above Torver vale, facing its yard and outbuildings, and its back turned to the glorious panorama of moor and mountain beyond the valley, cf. Lawson Park above Brantwood on the east side of Coniston Water.

## GRASSGUARDS
*Gressgards* 1599. 'Guards' is garth, as in Garth Nook, and is a common place name element in High Furness. A 'gressing' or 'grassing' was a grazing area on which a person was permitted to graze a specified quantity of stock.

## BRACKENBARROW
*Bracanbergh* in the charter quoted by Collingwood, *ut sup.*
*Brakenbarrowe* 1585.
Ekwall suggests that Sedbergh is O.N., meaning 'flat-topped hill'. Why then should Bracanbergh not be 'bracken-topped hill'? The farm is situated on the crest of a flattened ridge, or low mound, that runs north-south, and faces Grassguards instead of all the wild winds that blow off Old Man to the west (no doubt the reason why High Stile is similarly orientated). 'Bracken-covered mound' makes obvious topographical sense.

## HOATHWAITE
*Holthwaite* in a 13th-century grant to the Canons of Conishead Priory by Roger de Brackenbarrow, quoted, in translation, by West (*Antiquities of Furness*) from Dugdale's

*Monasticon Anglicanum*. The 'l' could be an error, because in the same section Torver appears as both 'Forferghe' and 'Thorsergh', and 'in Cumberland and Westmorland' forsooth.

*Hothwaite* 1603, *Howthwaite* 1614. A thwaite is a clearing in the forest that is used as meadow land, a place name element which occurs frequently in those parts of Furness colonised by the Scandinavians. The 'how' of 1614 combines with the 'thwaite' to make sound topographical sense.

## CHURCH HOUSE
*Kirkus* 1617. It seems a pity that the old spelling has not been retained. All the important Torver functions have taken place here, eg. meetings of the Court Baron and the autumn Shepherds' Meet.

## SATTERY LANE and CAR LANE
These are two old ways leading respectively to Moor and to Torver Park. Both names indicate the prevailing wetness of the valley floor.

## CROOK
*Crooke* 1703. 'Crook' is O.N. for a bend, say of a river, and Crook Farm is situated where Torver beck, having descended from the moor, bends round to run through the valley towards the mill.

## SCAR HEAD
*Scarhead* 1615. O.N. 'sker' means a rocky hill. Beyond Scar Head the road winds up to Tranearth and on to Walna Scar. The bare bones of the land are very much in evidence hereabouts, protruding through the grass, or gathered into walls. The cap fits.

## TRANEARTH
*Tranneth* 1836, *Tarnwath* 1849. Not even Ellwood had any suggestions for this one. Just below the house, above the confluence of Torver beck and Black beck, is a ford and the remains of a clapperbridge which crossed Torver beck from the road up to Eddy Scale quarry from Little Arrow. A clapperbridge consisted of a series of broad flagstones balanced on low stone piers to make a simple single-lane crossing of a stream. Little Arrow is in the no-man's land between Torver and Coniston, and the name was recorded in the charter quoted by Collingwood in his 'History' from the early 13th century as 'Litelherga', which looks suspiciously like 'little clearing'.

## BULL HAW MOSS
The O.N. 'mosi' means morass. A moss is an area of wet moorland which holds water like a sponge, a pretty exact description of the land below the Deer dyke on the High Common. It may be that 'Haw' was not always separate from 'Bull'. Local speakers run the two words together as 'Bulla', so that we could be dealing with a personal name.

## EDDY or ADDY SCALE
'Skali' is O.N. for a temporary building, say a hut situated on a summer pasture. 'Addy' could well be the name of the original Scandinavian settler.

## BANNISHEAD
The last element will be the O.N. 'saeter', a summer pasture. Just across the beck from Eddy Scale, higher on the moor, is the remains of an Iron Age homestead. 'Bannis' is another Scandinavian personal name, a byname this time, meaning 'the man who curses'. Let us hope that Addy managed to rub along with his excitable neighbour!

## TORVER PARK
There is no documentary evidence of land in Torver ever being emparked, and field work has revealed no trace of a park boundary.

## SOUTERSTEAD
*Sowtestead* 1614. This looks very like the O.N. word for sheep (cf. Soutergate in Ulverston), with 'stead', a farm.

## GREENRIGG
*Grenerigg* 1603, *Greinrige* 1612. The '-rigg' element is straightforward enough. 'Hyrggr' is O.S. for back, ridge, and is a common High Furness place name element. (cf. on Torver Low Common, Arne Riggs and Plain Riggs.) 'Grene' looks as if it should be 'green', which would fit very well, were it not for that alternative spelling, found again in 1635. Just possibly and without too much imaginative topography, it could be the O.N. 'grein' which indicates a fork of a river or a valley.

## HUMMERS
Hummers is the splendidly-named hill above Greenrigg, which slopes down to the main valley on its east side, and on the south to the beck which runs off Broughton Moor. Ellwood suggests that the name in fact means 'a grassy slope by the side of a river'.

## SEAL GILL
'Gil' is O.N. for a ravine, or narrow valley. (cf. Ash Gill on Torver High Common.) 'Seal' is the same word as 'sallies', willows, which still grow in this little cleft on the High Common above the Deer dyke.

## HARE CRAG
A circular earthwork, clearly not defensive, crowns this point of vantage above the valley. 'Horg' is O.N. for a heap of stones, or an altar. No less than ourselves, the first Scandinavian settlers must have felt the numinous atmosphere of this place.

## Note
*O.S. = Old Scandinavian, O.N. = Old Norse, O.E. = Old English*

*Appendix Two*

# The Three Churches of Torver

In Ellwood's *Forty Five Years in a Mountain Parish* is an illustration of the church as it had appeared before 1849. It is a small, low building, whitewashed, with a slated roof of fairly steep pitch. At the west end is a bell tower, not much higher than the apex of the main roof. Along the south side, moving from west to east, there is a simple slated porch, a square window, a low door, and finally, presumably lighting the chancel, two smaller square windows. The tower, also roofed with slate, is gabled on its east and west sides, the lines corresponding to the gables of the main building. Had it not been pulled down, but carefully cherished, this little church would now have been regarded as a gem of traditional Lakeland vernacular architecture.


In the same book is a picture of the second church, demolished in 1884. It is still a small building, but has been designed out of a textbook. The west tower is in three stages, marked by string courses, and has crenellation round the top. In the topmost stage are lancet-shaped openings for the bell chamber; in the middle one there is an Early English window, with hoodmould, looking west; in the lowest stage, also facing west, is the doorway, echoing the shape of the window, but broader. The body of the church, seen from the north in the drawing, is slated and stone built, like the tower, in the dark stone commonly used in these parts. Spaced along the north wall are five lancet-shaped lights, which rise from ground level. Each has what appears to be a relieving arch round its head just below the line of the roof. Inside, the 1849 church retained the three-decker pulpit from the older building. Ruskin evidently felt quite strongly about the incongruity between this church and its setting because, in the course of a letter to Ellwood on the architecture and appearance of Torver, he wrote that clergymen ought to understand that the old whitewashed churches were most in keeping with the surrounding scenery.

A note by Ellwood, dating from 1907, gives a scrap of information about the arrangements for public worship during the earlier part of his ministry which, besides being a testimony to his zeal, is also rather unusual. He records 'the gift by will of a small mountain chapel at Greenrigg, by Mrs. Airey, for use for divine service on Sundays. We had for five years uninterrupted service in this chapel on Sunday evenings.' The period must have been the mid-1870s, because in 1876 a Towers Charity prayer book was delivered to 'Greenrigg Chapel'. The room used for worship was on the upper floor of the slated, stone-built barn situated on the sloping ground close to the southern corner of the main house. Possibly the room, which measures 12ft. 9ins. by 16ft. 6ins., was originally a bracken store. A door gives direct access from the top level by the house, and a skylight provides modest illumination. On either side of the fireplace, inserted in the wall opposite the door, are shallow recesses, in which shelves would have accommodated hymnals and prayer books. The internal walls are plastered and whitewashed. In 1983 the room was used by Mrs. Myers for general storage purposes.

The existing church, dedicated to St Luke in 1884 when it was discovered that there had been no dedication hitherto, was designed by Messrs. Paley and Austin of Lancaster, also out of a textbook. It was, however, soundly constructed in a style regarded at the time as appropriate and acceptable, but not one to excite either the antiquarian or the aesthete of a century later. The visitor entering the church will note the plain sandstone font, dating probably from the 14th century. On the west wall are two large wooden panels on which have been painted the words of the Lord's prayer, the Apostles' creed and the Ten Commandments. This 19th-century work is a fairly late example of its type. The two lights in the west wall were installed in memory of Sarah Barratt, widow of William Barratt, in whose memory she herself had donated the windows above the altar. The Barratts of Holly How, Coniston, were then the principal landowners in Torver. There are two other commemorative windows, one on either side of the communion table, to the Rev. T. Ellwood and his faithful wife, Dorcas. All these windows are typically late Victorian both in conception and execution.

There are few wall plaques. The oldest dates from 1729, and is fixed to the south wall of the nave. It records the gift of John Woodvill, mariner, of Whitehaven: '15L to William Wilson and his heirs to dispose of for the use of the poor of Torver, as to paying for learning and books.' The small plaque in the north nave wall recalls the long ministry of Matthew Carter in the first half of the 19th century. Almost hidden in the passageway to the vestry is another plaque recording how in 1756 'this Church of Torver was augmented', and how in 1759 'lands were purchased with 400L, whereof 200L was given by Queen Anne's Bounty, 100L by the executors of William Stratford, and 100L by other benefactors'.

In the vestry the visitor can see the old oak parish chest, in use until the 1960s. On the lid, faint traces of geometrical decoration may still be seen. Set into the vestry walls are fragments of panelling from the old church. The initials incorporated in this work enable it to be dated from the early 18th century. 'T.B.' could refer to Thomas Birkett, who lived at Crook and was churchwarden in 1722, and 'M.C.' may be Matthew Coward, husbandman, of Oxenhouse, who was one of the apprizers of the will of John Park of Beckstones in 1724. Coward was never a churchwarden, however. Could it be that he and Birkett had been responsible for the carving? There is also an unusual old offertory box of oak, octagonal, eight inches across. Its handle, which terminates in an octagonal knob, is 10 inches long. Various initials have been scratched on this handle: 'E.W.' and 'W.W.' 1707 – presumably William Wilson of Greaves Ground and his wife Eleanor. It would be nice to think that they had given the box. Also inscribed are the initials of four clergymen, with dates: 'R.W.' 1734, 'R.B.' 1740, 'M.I.C.' 1807 and 'T.E.' 1861. It is a remarkable coincidence that these four who left their marks on this box each went on to an incumbency of extraordinary length, as if this initialling had been a passport to clerical longevity.

Hanging on the vestry wall is a framed drawing, prepared at the time when the present church was being built, to show the parishioners what they were going to have for their money. It is quite a good drawing, but the verdict of time must be that the exterior of the church is too uniformly dark and heavy. The central position of the squat tower seems to add to the feeling that, somehow, the whole building has never got off the ground. We may perhaps hope that the ancient yews which had witnessed two rebuildings in less than half a century felt that they were getting value this time. They at least remain as a living link with the oldest building of which we have any record on this site.

# Notes and References

**Chapter One**

1. A char is a fish rather similar to a trout in appearance, for which Coniston Water has long been renowned.

**Chapter Two**

1. *Transactions of the Cumberland and Westmorland Antiquarian and Archaeological Society*, vol. 9, 1888.
2. *The Stone Circles of the British Isles*, Yale University Press, 1976.
3. 'Cist' is really the same word as 'chest'. A burial cist such as the one described here would originally have been covered by a heap of rough stone 'cobbles' gathered from the fellside. Whether the stones were in turn covered by earth so as to make a smooth mound in an area where the soil cover varies between the thin and the non-existent, must remain a moot question.

**Chapter Three**

1. About fifty acres. A carucate was originally the quantity of land that could be ploughed by one ox-team in a season. Clearly this would vary in extent according to the locality and the nature of the soil, so in 1198 a carucate was fixed at 100 acres.
2. *Mort d'ancestor* was the name given to the procedure for determining a person's right to succeed to a piece of land in circumstances where the succession was disputed.
3. Conishead Priory, which had been founded in the reign of Henry II, was situated by the seashore to the south of Ulverston, near to the modern village of Bardsea.
4. *Novel Disseisin* was another of Henry II's arrangements for settling disputes relating to land tenure. This one was for dealing with complaints that a person had been wrongfully deprived of a piece of land. The idea behind it, as with *mort d'ancestor*, was to substitute the judgment of what we would call a jury for an old-fashioned trial of strength.
5. 'Soar' means a sorrel-coloured, and therefore a young, hawk. The Hodelestons, or Huddlestones, were for a long time the principal family in the Millom area.
6. These subsidies were the occasional grants made by medieval parliaments to meet extra-ordinary royal expenses, such as the cost of an important military campaign.

**Chapter Four**

1. A fee was a medieval benefice. It was originally the amount of land necessary to support a knight, who should be available at any time to go and serve his lord.

As time went on, a knight's fee came to have a conventional financial valuation, so that arrangements such as this one could be set out clearly and simply.
2. Baste is a fibrous material, part of the inner bark of trees.

## Chapter Five
1. Intake, still pronounced intak, is a piece of rough land enclosed from the adjacent moor.
2. Arnacrag, or Ornall Cragg means Eagle Crag, an interesting sidelight on the bird life in Torver during the Middle Ages.
3. A hoop was a local measure amounting to a quarter of a peck, as may be deduced from the following: an early 18th-century fragment records two transactions between the miller and Mary Parke, the one involving 'one peck of meall at 2s. 4d.', and the other 'three hoops of meall at 1s. 9d.'.
4. 'Skillings', according to Ellwood, were the farinaceous portion of wheat or oats separated from the husks, cf. Icelandic *skilja*, meaning 'to separate'.
5. Strong evidence of a continuing Scandinavian vocabulary is to be found in this phrase, used still in Sweden of, for example, a little boy who has failed to reach the lavatory in time.

## Chapter Six
1. In fact, the manor court records are now deposited in the Cumbria Record Office at Barrow in Furness. Walker transcribed a particularly full and interesting section. The 1585 and 1591 lists of jurymen are quite typical.
2. Muchland is Michael's Land. This manor, granted by William I to Sir Michael le Fleming, was based on Aldingham in Low Furness, and was originally known as the manor of Aldingham.
3. A hubbleshowe (spelling variable) is a disturbance or commotion. An alternative rendering of 'bloodwick' is 'bloodstroke', which is self-explanatory. Tuxhill looks as if it is intended as a synonym, or at any rate, a near relation of a hubbleshowe.
4. 'Leading' meant bringing down in a horse-drawn cart or sledge.
5. 100 rood, as a linear measure, = 550 yards. The Walna Scar road runs up from Coniston above the level of Banishead Moor, crosses Torver beck by Cove Bridge below Goat's Water, climbs to the pass between Walna Scar and Brown Pike and then drops down to Seathwaite in Dunnerdale. During the later 18th century the road was upgraded from a packhorse track to a bridlepath.
6. A sess was a rate levied equally on all householders for a particular purpose.
7. One rood = 5½ yards, or approximately 5 metres. However, from the payment to John Rigge (*see* Highway Accounts for 1778), it looks as if a Torver rood measured an inch or two less than 7 yards.
8. Mr. Bell was the parson.

## Chapter Eight
1. 'Arder' was a word used to mean 'ploughland'; perhaps ardor here means a growing crop.
2. ie. beasts, the word still used in Torver when referring to cattle.
3. Note how the horse and its 'furniture' heads the list.

4.   A wimble was used for making circular holes in the ground.
5.   This would be 50-60 sheep.
6.   Six or seven cattle.
7.   Peat, most likely.
8.   The actual measures, for holding a peck, or hoop, of meal etc.
9.   The horse heads the list again.
10.  Beasts. No more than four, probably, at £7 10s.

## Chapter Nine
1.   In those days 'natural' did not imply bastardy. But it does look as if Mary cut off her boys with the proverbial shilling.

## Chapter Ten
1.   The sconce could be moved to make a seat in front of the fire, so making a cosy room along with the side walls of the fire hood on cold winter nights.

## Chapter Eleven
1.   Also described, more accurately from the ecclesiastical point of view, as Parkground quarter.
2.   A commissary was an officer representing a bishop, and performing his duties in distant parts of the diocese. For many years at this period Dr. William Stratford was commissary for the area which included Torver.
3.   Churchwarden for 1743.
4.   [*sic.*] a general Torver usage in the 18th century.
5.   *Eiusdem* = 'of the same place'.
6.   *Idem* = 'the same man'.

## Chapter Twelve
1.   The Anabaptists were really the precursors of the Baptists. In the early days of the Reformation they had established a formidable reputation for their radical views and eccentric practices, and so it came about that even in the 18th century the Baptists were generally regarded with a greater degree of suspicion than any of the other dissenting sects.
2.   Stratford had for many years been secretary to Bishop Gastrell of Chester, author of the last book on the list, and commissary in the Archdeaconry of Richmond in that diocese. He was noted for his benevolence towards his fellow clergy.

## Chapter Fourteen
1.   The river is the man who rives, or splits, the thick slab of stone into thin slates, which are then dressed by means of a special heavy knife with a curved blade to the correct shape and size before being regularly lined up outside, pending their removal.
2.   These are the small branches brashed, or lopped, from the trunk of a tree to give it a cleaner appearance and a better shape for when it is eventually to be felled.
3.   A besom is a sweeping brush designed to be used out of doors. It consists of a bundle of whippy twigs, birch for example, fastened to the end of a long steel.

## Chapter Fifteen

1. Pinnel is the name given to the loose stony material, often fragmented, rotten, or shaly rock, that was used for repairing the roads.

## Chapter Seventeen

1. George Constantinesco, an internationally-famous engineer of Romanian birth, lived at Oxen House for many years. He is best known for his work on the device which enabled fighter pilots to fire a machine gun through the rotating blades of their propeller, during the First World War, and for his development of an infinitely varied gearing system for mechanically propelled vehicles. During the Second World War he was associated, *inter alia*, with the research which led to the production of 'bouncing' bombs.

# Index

# Index of People

Abington, Robert of, 17
Addyson, 23
Airey, 53, 120
Ambrose, 76
Appleyard, 110
Ascowe, 21
Ashburner, 23, 30
Askew, 46, 56
Atkinson, 21, 22, 23, 24, 25, 26, 30, 31, 32, 33, 45, 46, 49, 51, 52, 53, 55, 56, 63, 64, 66, 68, 74, 76, 81, 102

Bainbridge, 28
Bamford, 67
Barker, 23, 43
Barr, 109, 110
Barratt, 70, 79, 83, 105, 106, 121
Barrow, 106, 108, 110
Bayliff, 77
Bell, 30, 68, 76, 80
Benson, 49, 55
Biggins, 46, 103
Bigland, 33, 46, 49, 117
Birkett, 28, 30, 48, 51, 77-8, 81, 103, 104, 106, 121
Birrel, 30
Boyren, 113
Braithwaite, 34, 54
Breade, 102
Briggs, 53, 102
Brockbank, 31, 46, 51, 104, 109
Brocklebank, 26, 29, 30, 34, 45, 55, 103
Brown(e), 43, 47, 48, 49, 50, 51, 53, 56, 95
Brunskill, 102
Buccleugh, Elizabeth, Duchess of, 80
Bullock, 106
Butler, 103

Cann, *27*; 89
Carr, 25
Carter, 68, 70, 81, 102, 121
Casson, 46, 107
Chamley, 49, 50, 116

Charnley, 7, 93, 104, 105
Christoforson, 21
Clark, 104
Clayfe (Claife): Adam de, 14; William de, 14
Constantinesco, 113
Cookson, 102, 103
Copsie, 85
Coucy de, 14
Coulthard, 105, 106
Coward, 34, 81, 101, 106, 121
Cowper, 8, 9
Crabtree, 105
Cranmer, 63
Crewdson (Crowdson), 26, 45, 74, 81, 102, 103

Danson, 34, 51, 103
Dawson, 21, 34
Dickinson, 87
Dixon, 27, 31, 32, 54, 107
Dockray (Dockeray, Dockrey), 33, 103

Edwards, 110
Ellis, 13
Ellwood, 9, 68, 69, 70, 71, 75, 76, 77, 78, 81-3, 105, 106, 108, 116, 120, 121
Eskrigg, 51

Fearon, 28, 30, 33
Fitzgilbert, William, *see* Lancaster
Fitzreinfred, Gilbert, 12, 17, 115
Fleming, 19, 21, 28, 45, 49, 50, 51, 52, 53, 54, 55, 56, 66, 68, 75, 76, 81, 101, 102, 104
Furness, William de, 13

Garner, 49
Gibson, 32-3, 34, 103
Gillbank (Gillbanck, Gillbanks), 32-3, 56
Glaister, 108
Goodwin (Bishop of Carlisle), 71
Graves, 26

Gresdale, William de, 13
Grisedale, 86

Hall, 40, 65, 67, 68
Harrison, 32, 34, 49-50, 51, 104, 106
Hartley, 54, 112
Hartwell, 68
Haveryngton, John de, 14
Heaton (Hedon), 12-13, 14, 17, 71
Heelis, 83
High, 46, 53, 54
Higham, 68
Holroyd, 67
Horegrave, Henry de, 13
Huddleston (Hodeleston), 13, 17
Hudson, 104

Inman, *1*; 112

Jackson, 26, 33, 40, 45, 50, 51, 52, 55, 56, 64, 104, 109
Jenkinson, 49
Jones, 105

Kendal, 32, 86, 93, 103
Kendall, 79, 102, 108, 110
Kerby (Kirkby), 21, 33, 64

Lancaster, 21
Lancaster: William I de (Fitzgilbert), 11, 12, 17, 18; William II de, 12; William III de, 13
Leck, 52
Leech, 54
Lees, 49
Lindsay, 106
Low, 47
Lowther, 56, 76
Lund, 85
Lyon, 53

Machell, 33
Mandall, 70, 109
Massicks (Massacks), 83, 102, 104

130